The Book of Vishnu

The Book of
Vishnu

NANDITHA KRISHNA

PENGUIN BOOKS

PENGUIN BOOKS
Published by the Penguin Group
Penguin Books India Pvt. Ltd, 11 Community Centre, Panchsheel Park,
New Delhi 110 017, India
Penguin Group (USA) Inc., 375 Hudson Street, New York, New York
10014, USA
Penguin Group (Canada), 90 Eglinton Avenue East, Suite 700, Toronto,
Ontario, M4P 2Y3, Canada (a division of Pearson Penguin Canada Inc.)
Penguin Books Ltd, 80 Strand, London WC2R 0RL, England
Penguin Ireland, 25 St Stephen's Green, Dublin 2, Ireland (a division of
Penguin Books Ltd)
Penguin Group (Australia), 250 Camberwell Road, Camberwell, Victoria
3124, Australia (a division of Pearson Australia Group Pty Ltd)
Penguin Group (NZ), 67 Apollo Drive, Rosedale, North Shore 0632, New
Zealand (a division of Pearson New Zealand Ltd)
Penguin Group (South Africa) (Pty) Ltd, 24 Sturdee Avenue, Rosebank,
Johannesburg 2196, South Africa

Penguin Books Ltd, Registered Offices: 80 Strand, London WC2R 0RL,
England

First published in Viking by Penguin Books India 2001
Published in Penguin Books 2009

ISBN 9780143067627

Typeset in Sabon by Mantra Virtual Services, New Delhi
Printed at Saurabh Printers Pvt. Ltd, Noida

Contents

Introduction

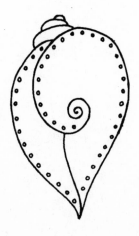

The Supreme God of the Hindus is Brahman, the Absolute Universal Soul. The entire cosmos is a manifestation of him and it is from him that all forms of life evolved. He is formless, without qualities, neither male nor female, and infinite, without beginning or end. He is found within us and around us, and the goal of every Hindu is to shake off the karmic cycle of birth, death and rebirth and attain moksha (nirvana or liberation), which is unity with the Supreme Soul.

To make the formless or Nirguna Brahman comprehensible to the average person, he takes the form of the Saguna Brahman with form and attributes. This is the great god Ishwara, on whom we can fix our minds, pray and meditate. When Ishwara creates the universe, he is called Brahma; when he protects, he is called Vishnu; and when he destroys evil, he is called Shiva. The three together form the Trinity or Trimurti who control the universe and its functions. But whereas Brahma the Creator is less an object of popular worship and is, rather, associated with the development of philosophy, Shiva and Vishnu claim large cult followings and, along with Devi and a few other gods such as Ganesha and Kartika, are the popular deities of contemporary Hinduism.

In popular Hinduism, Vishnu is the Preserver, the protector of the good and the guardian of Dharma, the law of righteousness and the moral order. He is Narayana (the resting-place of souls), Parama Bhagavata (the Supreme Being) and Aja (the Unborn One). He is benevolent and reigns in Vaikuntha, the highest heaven and the goal of the pious. As protector, he is regarded as a bhoga murti, one who rewards his devotees. In an age of materialism, this increases his popularity several-fold.

Vishnu may be depicted as standing or seated, astride or beside his vehicle, Garuda, the eagle. He may also be depicted as Narayana, resting or seated on his couch Adi Shesha or Ananta, the many-hooded serpent, in the primeval waters. He is generally four-armed, holding the shankha (conch), chakra (discus), gada (club) and padma (lotus), although certain forms of Vishnu may have more, or less, arms and attributes. His consort is Lakshmi or Shridevi, the goddess of prosperity, who emerged from the primordial waters, seated on the lotus and holding a lotus. Sometimes Vishnu is depicted with a second consort, Bhudevi or the earth mother.

The most important aspect of Vishnu is his ability to incarnate himself on earth whenever Dharma is in danger, to save good from evil. The incarnation may be human, anthropomorphic or animal. In popular perception Vishnu has ten incarnations, of which the last is yet to be born. Of the incarnations, two—Rama and Krishna—are the subjects of India's two great epics, the *Ramayana* and the *Mahabharata*, and command their own devotees. Their popularity has contributed greatly to the growth of Vishnu and the Vaishnava sect.

Vishnu Narayana

Vishnu

Vishnu is an ancient god who first appears in the Rig Veda as an Aditya or solar deity, the son of Aditi, the mother of the gods. Early Vedic religion was intensely pantheistic in nature and all the devas or 'shining ones' (the word would come to mean gods much later) were aspects of natural forces over which the people had no control. Vedic gods were generally solar in nature, the sun being the source of all life on earth.

The Rig Vedic Vishnu is a manifestation of light, whose head was, by a trick of the gods, severed from his body and became the sun. He is the creator of the solar year: like a rounded wheel, he sets in motion his 'ninety racing steeds and the four', says the Veda. Here the steeds represent the days in each season and the 'four', the four seasons themselves.

Vishnu's unique quality in the Rig Veda is his ability to stride through the universe in three steps. Man knows the first two positions where he places his foot, for they are the positions of the rising and setting sun. But Vishnu alone knows the third place, the highest point in the firmament, and the position of the midday sun. This is the abode of the pious dead to which his devotees aspire, the goal of all spiritual attainment. The dust raised by his footsteps forms the rays of the sun that envelop the world. By striding thus, he holds up the sky and maintains the cosmic order.

In the Veda, Vishnu is a friend and associate of Indra, god of rain, thunder and storm. Together, Vishnu the sun and Indra the rain, take on the demon Vritra, the drought. Indra and Vishnu are alternately described as Vritrahan or the killer of Vritra. The story of drought in India is as old as Indian civilization. Further, this was a period when the river Saraswati in western India was gradually drying up and the desert was advancing. In the circumstances, the sun was invoked to unleash the rain and provide devotees with a bountiful harvest.

Vishnu is also the protector of the sacrifice in the Rig Veda. He is the sacrifice, he obtains its fruits, and he averts the evil consequences of defects in the sacrifice. In the Brahmanic period, when sacrifices became paramount, this was an important quality that contributed to Vishnu's position as the Supreme God. A story in the Shatapatha Brahmana describes how Vishnu attained the position of the Supreme God. The devas held a sacrificial session. It was decided that the deity who, by virtue of his deeds, completed the sacrifice first should be deemed the highest of the gods. Vishnu attained the end first and was therefore given the supreme position.

The Rig Vedic Vishnu is associated with the mountains, as girikshit and girishtha. This connection is not very clear, as the popular perception of the god is either pastoral or aquatic.

While most of the prominent deities of early Vedic religion were relegated to minor roles as the religion developed, Vishnu grew in popularity and strength till he became one of the most powerful gods of Hinduism.

His rapid growth in stature was due to his benevolent nature, the seed of which is to be found in the Rig Veda itself. Vishnu means all-pervading: he is the all-pervading sun, whose rays envelope the earth, who protects the sacrifice and sends forth the rain and is the final abode of the pious dead. He is invoked to bestow wealth, welfare, possessions and protection. He takes his three strides to secure his people. Benevolence, goodwill and willingness to help his devotees whenever they call upon him are characteristics that made Vishnu popular in an increasingly material world and which brought him into the world in several incarnations. His name Vasu itself means wealth, and he is identified with gold, the colour of the sun. He is also the lord of cattle, a symbol of wealth.

Along with Brahma the Creator and Shiva the Destroyer, Vishnu the Preserver became one of the Trinity and, for ardent Vaishnavas, the Supreme God Himself.

Narayana

An important aspect of Vishnu is Narayana, the resting place of departed souls. This quality appears in the Rig

Vedic description of the 'paramam padam', the third resting place of his foot, the highest point in the sky, the goal of pious souls. Narayana lies on the waters. Out of his navel grows a lotus, on which is seated the Creator Brahma. When evil is destroyed after each yuga and the earth is plunged into darkness and floods, Narayana creates a new world and gives people the opportunity to be good again. He may lie on the waters represented by the multi-hooded cobra or, in the form of a small child, float on a leaf on the water.

Narayana is more complex than Vishnu. The name Narayana itself first appears in the Satapatha Brahmana, although not in connection with Vishnu. The Narayana form of the god was unknown to the early Vedas, while his character evolves much later, in the epic period. The *Mahabharata* tells us that he had given the waters the name *nara* and as they are his abode, he is called Narayana. But water in Sanskrit is *aapa*. *Neera* or *neeru* is the common word for water in all the Dravidian languages. Again, *ayana* is described as abode. But the Sanskrit word for abode is *ayatana*. In the Dravidian languages, the meaning of *aya* is 'to lie' or 'to lose consciousness as in sleep', while *an* is the male personal termination.

Thus Narayana appears to be a non-Vedic deity with Dravidian origins who was combined with the Vedic Vishnu.

The Atharva Veda speaks of a great Yaksha in the midst of creation, lying upon the sea in penance, with the gods set therein like the branches of a tree. This Yaksha who knows the reed of God is the mysterious Lord of Life. This is the earliest description of a figure resembling the Narayana of later literature and of the tree of creation. Yakshas were non-Vedic gods and spirits connected with nature worship. They lived in plants and water and were popular in Buddhism and Jainism. Although they disappeared from later religion, they live on in local sects and traditions.

At the time of the great flood, the mahapralaya, Rishi Markandeya was traversing the vast expanse of the waters which had destroyed everything on earth. He came across a small child resting on the branch of a tree. Amazed at the sight, the holy sage asked the child to identify himself. 'Long ago, I gave the waters the name Nara. Because they have always been my abode, I am called Narayana.' Narayana then took credit for the creation, preservation and destruction of the universe. The motif of a child floating on a leaf is still seen in popular art. Many ancient Tamil tribes and dynasties claimed origin from this form of Narayana. These stories, along with other evidence suggest that Narayana was a non-Vedic deity of the waters who was combined with the solar Vishnu of the Vedas to form a composite God, who was to become one of the most powerful deities of Hinduism. The combination of the two—Vishnu and Narayana—contributed to the popularity and growth of the deity.

Links outside India

The link between the Vedic Aryans and the ancient Iranians is well known. According to the Zoroastrian Gathas, which follow the Vedic period, Verethraghna, the 'victor over adverse attack', was born in the ocean and had ten incarnations: the wind, bull, horse, camel, wild boar, fifteen year old youth, raven, ram, buck and perfect hero. The name Veretraghna is similar to the Vedic Vritrahan, a name shared by Indra and Vishnu. Vritra in the Rig Veda is the demon of drought, and Vritrahan is the destroyer of the drought, an appellation of Indra, the rain, and Vishnu, the sun.

Ancient Egyptians worshipped Horus, the morning sun. Together with the all-powerful Ra, the midday sun, and Atum, the setting sun, he formed a triad. Horus-Ra was portrayed as a divine child born each morning from the primeval waters, seated on a lotus whose petals enfolded him when the sun set every night. Atum originated as a serpent in the primordial waters of Nu. The trio is represented by Ra, his falcon head framed by a solar disc surrounded by a serpent; Horus as a crew-member traversing the skies in a boat formed by a snake,

Atum. The imagery is very reminiscent of the descriptions of the three steps of the Vedic Vishnu, as well as Padmanabha, the form of Narayana lying on the waters with the lotus issuing out of his navel. In the Indian tradition, Brahma, the Creator, is seated on the lotus.

The similarity with a Babylonian story of creation from Nippur is also remarkable. Enki, god of the waters, lies in deep sleep at the bottom of the ocean. The gods complain to him about the lack of bread, but he does not hear them. Then his mother Nammu, the mother of the gods, wakes him and tells him to go forth and create man. Enki has the head of a snake and the tail of a fish. The fish is one of the incarnations of Vishnu and the serpent is his couch. Enki's wife is Ninki, the goddess of the waters: Vishnu's consort is Lakshmi who was born from the ocean.

Vaikuntha

This is Vishnu's heaven, the goal to which all mortals aspire. It is the ultimate paradise where everything is perfect. Sometimes it is identified with Mount Meru, the centre of the universe, sometimes it is called the Northern Ocean. It is also called Vaibhra. Vishnu is the Lord of Paradise, or Vaikunthanatha.

The eagle and the snake

The Adiparva of the *Mahabharata* has an elaborate story to explain the association of the eagle and the snake with Vishnu and their mutual enmity. Kadru and Vinata, two daughters of Prajapati, were married to Rishi Kashyapa. Granted a boon by their husband, Kadru asked for a thousand powerful Nagas (snakes) as her sons, while Vinata asked for two sons, equal in strength, energy, size and prowess to all the thousand sons of Kadru.

After a long time, Kadru gave birth to one thousand eggs and Vinata two. They were kept separately in warm vessels for five hundred years, when the sons of Kadru were born. But Vinata's eggs did not produce anything. Ashamed, Vinata broke open one egg and a half-formed embryo with its upper part developed came out and, for prematurely breaking the egg, cursed her with five thousand years of slavery to her sister Kadru. Then the child became Aruna (dawn), the charioteer of the Sun, and is seen early every morning, shielding the earth from the Sun's heat.

Meanwhile, when the ocean was churned for amrita, the nectar of immortality (see chapter on Kurma, the Tortoise), one of its many products was the beautiful and powerful horse Uchaishrava. Kadru and Vinata had a wager about its colour. Vinata said it was white, Kadru said it had a black tail. The loser would become the slave of the winner. Kadru asked her Naga sons to cover the horse's tail, that it may appear black. When they refused, she cursed them to die in the snake sacrifice that Janamejaya of the Pandavas would perform. Worried, the Nagas decided to become black hairs on the horse's tail, and Vinata thus became Kadru's slave.

Five thousand years passed and Vinata's second egg burst open, revealing Garuda, a bird of great splendour and strength, who soared into the sky in search of his natural food, snakes. But he, along with his mother was forced to serve the Nagas. When he asked the Nagas for the price of their freedom, they demanded amrita, the nectar of immortality. Garuda fought the devas and took away the nectar, but did not drink it himself. Pleased with Garuda's self-denial, Vishnu granted him immortality, freedom from disease and a position on the flag-staff of his chariot, above the god.

Indra granted Garuda's desire that snakes should become his food, and Vishnu took away the nectar when Garuda placed it on the ground. Thus Garuda freed his mother from slavery, the snakes became his food and were denied immortality.

Of the Nagas, the eldest, Shesha or Ananta, hearing his mother's curse, went all over the country, practising austere penances and meditating. When approached by Brahma, he lamented that his brothers had wicked hearts and were envious of Vinata and her son Garuda, so he desired to cast off his body and live a virtuous life forever. Granting him his wish, Brahma also commanded him to hold the earth steady. For upholding the earth, Ananta became Dharma. Ananta was so powerful that he alone could uproot the Mandara mountain for the churning of the ocean.

Ananta means infinite and represents the endlessness of cosmic time, while his thousand hoods represent the innumerable divisions of time. The word shesha means remainder and represents that which is left over from the previous creation, which forms the seed for the next.

Garuda the eagle is the vahana or vehicle of Vishnu. In the Rig Veda he is an associate of Indra and the sun. The visual image of a huge bird with widespread wings flying out of the sky would have contributed to this association. Many civilizations have used the symbol of the eagle to represent the majesty, power and remoteness of the sun.

The enmity between Garuda and the Nagas is the enmity between the forces of light and darkness. Garuda and Aruna represent the sun and light, the Nagas night and darkness. Although darkness tries to swallow the light, light is immortal, giving and protecting existence. It is the divine Vishnu, the sun himself.

The attributes

Vishnu is usually depicted with four arms, though sometimes he is shown with eight or even sixteen. In his hands he holds the shankha (conch), chakra (disc), gada (club), padma (lotus) and, occasionally, the khadga (sword) and sharanga (bow).

The many arms of Hindu deities are symbolic of the gods' manifold powers. Whereas a mere mortal has limited abilities, a god's power is unlimited, represented by the many arms that hold a variety of attributes and perform myriad activities, often simultaneously.

Vishnu's attributes are of an evolutionary order, from the club (gada), used in hand-to-hand warfare, to the chakra (boomerang), a weapon that is thrown and from the shankha (conch), a war trumpet, to the padma (lotus), a symbol of creation and purity.

Vishnu's attributes were actually weapons of Rama and Krishna. The weapons are important in that they represent the evolution of the deity along with the evolution of the people who worshipped him. In fact, they are studies in Indian anthropology, with each attribute narrating a stage in the evolutionary process of the god and, thereby, his people. The contemporary celebration of the Ganesha festival in Maharashtra provides an interesting illustration of this process. Today's Ganeshas carry guns, kalishnikovs and nuclear-headed missiles, or sit in front of a computer. Similarly, Vishnu was given the weapons and instruments popular with his worshippers.

Gada

Vishnu's mace is called the Kaumodaki. It sounded like thunder and was capable of killing the daityas and was given to him by Varuna, lord of the waters. The name Kaumodaki is derived from the water lily plant, the Kumuda.

Of all weapons known to man, the mace or club is the oldest. Initially made from a thick log of wood and later of stone, it was the popular weapon of the Neolithic period. There is no civilization where it was not known: mace heads appeared in India as early as 10,000 BC in Mohenjo Daro. The association of the mace with Vishnu suggests that the god would have been worshipped by a Neolithic people in the course of his evolution.

In the philosophical development of Vaishnavism, the mace represents the intellect, the power of knowledge and the power of time. Just as time is unconquerable, the mace destroys those who oppose it.

There are several names for the mace in Sanskrit literature, but the importance of the mace can be gauged by the fact that an entire book of the *Mahabharata*—the Gadaparva—is named after this weapon. The Pandava prince Bhima and his Kaurava cousin Duryodhana were experts in mace combat, and Duryodhana, the king of Hastinapura, was killed by Bhima's mace. Krishna's brother Balarama is also an expert in wielding the mace, and it is the weapon of Rama's monkey allies, the Vanaras. Gods and demons alike use this mighty weapon of war.

Shankha

There are several versions of how Krishna obained his conch Panchajanya. A story in the *Mahabharata* says that Krishna obtained the conch after killing the demon Panchajana who lived in the depths of Patala (modern Hyderabad, Sindh). The Vishnu Purana and Harivamsa have different versions. After completing their education with Guru Sandipani, Krishna and Balarama asked their teacher to name his fee. Sandipani asked for his son Punardatta, who had been kidnapped by Panchajana of the Punyajana or Pani tribe from Prabhasa (modern Prabhas, near Somnath in Gujarat). Panchajana used the conch as a war trumpet (another version says that Panchajana lived in a conch under the waters). He had sold Punardatta to the matriarchial Naga Queen of Vaivasvatapuri (city of light) near Patala. Krishna killed Panchajana and acquired his conch, hence its name Panchajanya, and returned Punardatta to his father Guru

Sandipani. When Krishna was identified with Vishnu, the conch became an emblem of Vishnu.

The Panis or Punyajana were traders, described by the Rig Veda as demons, usurers and even Dasyus (enemies) of hostile speech. They have been identified with the ancient sea-faring Phoenicians. Panchajana's aides, Hukku and Hulla, are described as speaking a strange tongue and having been brought up in a 'lonely desert far across the sea'. The Pani or Punyajana tribe had captured Kushasthali (modern Dwaraka). By killing Panchajana, their leader, Krishna regained Dwaraka. The acquisition of the Panchajanya conch, symbol of Panchajana, is symbolic of Krishna's victory.

The conch or chank shell is the shell of the gastropod *Mollusc turbinella rapa* which is found in the sea off Gujarat and in the Gulf of Mannar. A well-developed industry manufacturing shell jewellery existed as early as 2500 BC, while the conch was an article of trade. Later Vedic literature refers to the blowing of the conch at ceremonies, a common function even today, while the *Ramayana* and *Mahabharata* describe its use to assemble warriors and to create the atmosphere for a war.

The conch itself is not sacred: it is the divinity of Vishnu that makes it sacred. The story of Krishna's acquisition of the symbol from Panchajanya suggests that it was an emblem—like a totem—of the demon. As

Krishna defeats the demon, he acquires the demon's emblem, again a totemic association, for the victor acquires the totem of the defeated tribe or warrior. The likelihood of a totemic association is reinforced by the fact that the conch is the symbol of the Jaina Tirthankara Neminatha, son of Samudravijaya, king of Dwaraka in Gujarat. Each Tirthankara is identified with a totem-like emblem, an animal, a plant or a natural object (like the conch). Also, the shankha's association with the waters reinforces its association with Narayana, who rests on the waters.

In later literature, the conch is symbolic of the elements, derived from the separation of ahankara (egoism), or the principle of consciousness, into a twofold division of sense and elements. The vibrations of the shankha represent the material creative force. Apart from the five elements (earth, air, water, fire and space), three more properties are derived from space (akasha): mind (mana), intellect (buddhi) and egoism (ahankara). In Vishnu's hand the shankha represents space, a manifestation of sound, the origin of the elements and the creative force. It is one of the nine treasures of Kubera, the god of wealth, and grants wishes and wealth. It is used in the sacred ritual bath of the deity and in the consecration of a new temple and is blown during important festivals.

Chakra

As the gods and the demons churned the ocean to gain
the nectar of immortality, Vishnu thought of his fiery
and destructive chakra, which came into his hands and
destroyed demons by the thousands. The *Mahabharata*
says that Shiva created the chakra after he killed a demon
who lived in the waters. Blazing with fire and energy,
only Shiva could look at it, hence its name Sudarshana
('wonderful vision'). While there is no further explanation
for this story, many of the tribes and asuras who
challenged Krishna's chakra with their own chakras were
Shaivites. This could be yet another instance of the victor
appropriating the weapon of his defeated enemies.
According to another story, Krishna worshipped Agni
the god of fire, in the Khandva forest. Pleased, Agni
gave him the fiery Sudarshana chakra to decimate his
enemies.

The chakra is first described as a 'sharp' weapon of
war in the Rig Veda. But it is not a common weapon.
Like the shankha, the chakra is popular only in the epic
period. It is used by Krishna, the devas and the asuras.
Krishna used the chakra to behead the planet Rahu and
the prince Shishupala, to defeat the demons Madhu and
Kaitabha and to destroy the armies of Rukmin and
Jarasandha. The word chakra means wheel, although
Vishnu's chakra is generally translated as discus.

The distinguishing feature of the chakra is its ability to return to the hand of he who throws it. Time and again it is hurled by Krishna, destroys the enemy, sometimes entire armies and kingdoms, and returns to him. Although the chakra has been described as the discus, the only weapon known to have this quality is the boomerang.

The boomerang is a Neolithic weapon. While the aboriginal tribes of Australia are its best-known users, several ancient people between Eritrea, Sumeria and Gujarat used a boomerang-like weapon. The Sumerians used a circular boomerang, not unlike the Pallava representations of Vishnu's chakra. The Indian tribes used both circular and crescent-shaped boomerangs. In India, the Kolis of Gujarat, the Maravars and Kallars of Tamil Nadu and some other Adivasi tribes used similar weapons.

Later, the Vishnu Purana identifies the chakra with the mind 'whose thoughts, like the weapon, flew faster than the wind'. The Bhagavata Purana describes the chakra as possessing the qualities of prana (life principle), maya (illusion), kriya (activity), shakti (energy), bhava (emotion), unmera (ideals), udyama (exertion) and sankalpa (will). The chakra is invoked in Tantric rites, and a chakra held in a person's hand is the symbol of a universal emperor or chakravartin.

Padma

When Narayana contemplated the creation of mankind, a lotus sprang out of his navel. Seated on it was the four-headed Creator, Brahma, illuminating all the directions with his brightness. Narayana was given the name Padmanabha or lotus-navel.

The lotus that lit up the sky with its effulgence was identified with the sun. As the first creation of the Supreme Being Narayana, the lotus became a symbol of creation and, thereby, fertility. As it arose from the ocean, it represented the waters, the source of all life and also Dharma, the cosmic law. By growing away from the dirt and impurity of the sea bed in which demons and serpents dwell, the lotus became a symbol of purity. So also the individual soul, though rooted in an imperfect world, searches for perfection.

The lotus in Vishnu's hand also represents Lakshmi, the goddess of prosperity who is seated on a lotus and also holds one in one or both hands. The lotus is the creative force, generating cosmic action. It is the feminine principle that activates the creative power of the Supreme Being, like the yin and the yang or Shiva and Shakti.

Khadga

Occasionally, Vishnu holds the sword or khadga.

However, apart from an allusion to Rama's sword in the *Ramayana*, there is nothing to tell us how and why Vishnu obtained it. It also appears very rarely in iconography.

The sword first appears in the coins of the Greek kshatrapas (satraps) of north-west India. Alexander's Greek soldiers wielded the sword and it obviously entered the country with them. Its association with Vishnu begins as late as the Gupta period, suggesting that its success in the hands of the Greeks made it a weapon to be respected.

Sharanga

Just as Krishna's shankha and chakra are associated with Vishnu, Rama's bow and arrow are also associated with the deity. The sharanga (bow) is not an important or frequently seen weapon of Vishnu and seems to have become his possession when the cult of Rama was identified with him.

Iconography

While the earliest extant image of Vishnu is probably a four-armed figure holding the shankha, chakra and gada from Malhar in Madhya Pradesh, dating back to 200 BC, Vishnu images are prolific in the Kushana period (AD 200). Most icons are four-armed and hold the shankha, chakra, gada and padma. His consort Lakshmi, represented as Shridevi and Bhudevi—the sky and the earth respectively—stands on either side of the god. Sometimes Lakshmi is also represented as the shrivatsa, a symbol of Devi that Vishnu carries on his chest. While the early figures are crowned or wear a headdress, later images wear the tall kirita, a symbol of divinity.

Standing images of Vishnu may or may not have Garuda beside him, but Vishnu generally sits on the eagle, just as he reclines on the snake, a symbol of the waters.

Later Vishnu icons are of three types: standing or sthanaka murtis, seated or asana murtis and resting or shayana murtis. Each may be of any one of four types: yoga for meditation, bhoga for giving boons, vira for the warrior and abhicharika for Tantric ritual. The attributes he holds and the gods, sages and attendants who surround him, define each type. Each type may be further divided into three categories: highest (uttama), intermediate (madhyama) and lowest (adhama) depending on whether they fulfil all, some or none of the requirements.

The iconography of Vishnu as we now know him first appears in the Kushana period. But it was the Gupta period that saw a profusion of Vishnu images. Special mention must be made of the temple at Deogarh in Madhya Pradesh. Here Vishnu can be seen as Nara-Narayana, a unique relief of the duo of Nara and

Narayana communicating, one listening and the other advising; as Gajendra Rakshaka (protector), a majestic image of Vishnu swooping down, seated on a flying Garuda, to save his devotee Gajendra, the elephant, from the crocodile demon. He is seated on his vehicle, the magnificent flying Garuda, and reclines on Adi Shesha, his bed in the ocean, with personifications of his attributes—the ayudha purushas—on a panel beneath.

Incarnations

From time to time, evil overpowers good and the earth comes to be ruled by wicked kings and demons who deny the rule of Dharma, the cosmic law of righteousness. They suppress virtue and morality till life on earth becomes unbearable. Only the truly devout survive and they put their faith in their god. In response to their prayers, Vishnu incarnates himself again and again as an avatara, to put an end to adharma, or unrighteousness, and restore order on earth. It is believed that he has manifested himself nine times, with the tenth or final incarnation yet to come. Some texts enumerate more, with the Bhagavata Purana mentioning twenty-two incarnations, but ten is the most popular number.

The avataras are, in order:

- Matsya, the fish
- Kurma, the tortoise

- Varaha, the boar
- Narasimha, the man-lion
- Vamana, the dwarf
- Parashurama, Rama with the axe
- Rama, the perfect man
- Krishna, the philosopher king
- Buddha, the preacher of peace
- Kalki, the final destroyer.

Each incarnation is relevant to the place, people and period. Interestingly, there is an evolutionary order among them, starting with the aquatic fish, developing into the amphibious tortoise, the four-legged animal and finally the two-legged human being. Besides these avataras or incarnations, Vishnu also manifests himself in different forms in different places. Each temple of the god has a unique story or sthala purana.

The incarnations correspond with the yugas or ages of life on earth. Each age is preceded by a period of twilight or sandhya.

The first four incarnations occur in the age of Satya (truth) or Krita (purity) yuga, a golden age.

The next age or Treta yuga commenced with the Vamana or dwarf incarnation. Sacrifices were carried out, and people were truthful and good. But righteousness decreased and people performed rites and gave gifts in order to receive rewards, not out of duty.

Dharma decreased further in the Dwapara yuga,

when Krishna was born. Some men studied four Vedas, others three, two, one or even none at all. Disease, desire and calamities struck the world. Some people offered sacrifices to overcome them while others practiced severe austerities.

The last age or Kali yuga began during the *Mahabharata* war. Dharma practically ceases to exist. Calamities and disease, poverty and hunger, violence and fear stalk the earth. The tenth incarnation of Vishnu, Kalki, will destroy the human race.

There is a difference of opinion as to whether Buddha was an incarnation of Vishnu, particularly since he was highly inimical to Vedic tradition. The alternative then is Balarama, Rama of the plough and elder brother of Krishna, who is listed after Rama, thereby removing Buddha and making Krishna the ninth incarnation. The inclusion of the Buddha was obviously done to integrate a popular school of belief into Hinduism.

While all other incarnations are partial—involving only a specific ability of Vishnu required to respond to a specific need—Krishna alone is a full avatara, the incarnation of Vishnu in his entirety on earth.

The promise of reincarnation has made it possible for several local deities to be identified with Vishnu. His numerous manifestations are the answer to every believer's prayer, for he sees in his local deity a form of Vishnu. As Krishna promises in the Bhagavad Gita:

Yadaa yadaa hi dharmasya glaanirbhavati
    bhaarata;
Abhyutthaanam adharmasya tadaatmaanam
    srujaamyaham.
Paritraanaaya saadhoonaam vinaashaaya cha
    drushkrutaam;
Dharma sansthaapanaarthaaya sambhavaami
    yuge yuge.

Which means:

'Whenever righteousness declines and unrighteousness prevails, I manifest Myself; For the protection of the good, for the destruction of the wicked and for the establishment of righteousness, I am born in every age.' (Bhagavad Gita, IV. 8)

It is this promise that the devotee sees Vishnu redeeming when he takes on a new incarnation or manifestation. This also makes it possible for a multiplicity of local deities to be identified with Vishnu and, thereby, be absorbed into the Hindu pantheon.

Matsya, the Fish

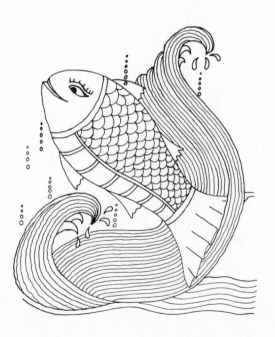

As the Matsya avatara, Vishnu saves Manu, the progenitor of mankind, the Sapta Rishis (seven sages) and their wives and one of every form of creation during the earth-destroying deluge. It is these survivors who later repopulate the world. Initially, in the Shatapatha Brahmana, the fish is identified with Brahma: later, it is regarded as an incarnation of Vishnu.

According to the *Mahabharata*, one day, when Manu was performing his religious rituals on the banks of the river Cherivi, a little fish came up to him and said that were Manu to take care of him, then he, Manu, would be saved from the deluge. He instructs Manu to keep him in a jar to protect him from other fish. Then, when he outgrows the jar he asks to be put in a tank. When he outgrows the tank, he wants to be taken to the river Ganga and, thereafter, to the ocean. There, Manu is to build a ship and board it when the floods begin.

Manu did as he was told. When the deluge began, he tied the ship to the fish who steered him through the violent storm towards the northern mountains. Eventually, the ship reached the peak of the Himalayas. Manu stepped out and descended the mountain and beheld a desolate world. The flood had swept away all living creatures: Manu alone was left. The fish then identified himself as the Lord of all creatures, Brahma. He gave Manu the power to create, and thus Manu took up the work of creation.

The Bhagavata Purana narrates a different tale. Long ago, when life first appeared on earth, a terrible demon called Hayagriva or Somaka terrorized the earth. He prevented the holy sages from performing their rituals and stole the Vedas, which he hid in the depths of the ocean. Brahma approached Vishnu for help and the latter immediately assumed the form of a fish and plunged into the ocean. He killed the demon and brought back the Vedas.

The Matsya Purana (named after this incarnation) contains yet another version of this story.

At the end of the kalpa (the duration of the world, or four thousand, three hundred and twenty million mortal years), while Brahma was resting, the demon Hayagriva stole the Vedas. When Vishnu discovered this, he took the form of a tiny fish. One day, when Satyavrata, the king of Dravida desha, was offering water in his cupped hands to the souls of his ancestors, he found this tiny fish in his hands. The little fish begged him to save it from the predators of the sea. Feeling great compassion, Satyavrata placed it in a pot. The next morning, he found that it had grown as large as the pot and thus, he ordered it to be placed in a well. The following morning it was as wide as the well, so the king transferred it into a tank. But still it grew, till it was as large as the tank. The king then told his men to take it to the sea. But even the sea was not large enough and the fish filled it from one shore to another.

Amazed, the king asked the fish to identify itself and explain why it was growing so large. The fish revealed himself as Vishnu and proclaimed that a great deluge—a mahapralaya—would flood the earth for a period of one hundred years. The king was instructed to keep one of each species of animal, all medicinal plants and seeds in a boat, with the Vedas above them. Thereafter, the fish told him to attach the boat to his fins with a rope made of a large snake. When the rains began, they came down so heavily that the entire world was submerged. The great flood continued ceaselessly for a hundred years. In all that time, Satyavrata and his boat were kept afloat by the great fish. Finally, when the waters receded, the creatures in the boat went back to creating new lives. And thus the world and creation began anew.

This story is very similar to the story of Noah in the Old Testament of the Bible, with the addition of the fish and the saving of the divine Vedas. The oldest recorded story of a great flood is to be found in Babylonian tablets. The story appears in the annals of every ancient civilization in Asia, Australasia, Europe and the Americas. It was obviously an actual event that has stayed in the memory of mankind.

At the end of the pralaya, Vishnu went back to his heaven Vaikuntha, without instructing people about the worship of the Matsya form or the construction of temples for it. Hence there are very few temples for this incarnation. The two best known are the Shankhodara temple at Bet Dwarka in Gujarat and the Vedanarayana temple at Nagalapuram in Andhra Pradesh. Matsya is generally represented as a four-armed figure with the upper torso of a man and the lower torso of a fish. Only occasionally is he represented as a full fish.

The fish incarnation also represents the earliest form of life, which began in water.

Kurma, the Tortoise

On the evolutionary scale, the next form of life would be amphibian, one that can survive on both land and water. This is represented by Kurma, the tortoise, the second incarnation of Vishnu.

The story of this manifestation of Vishnu appears in the *Ramayana* and several of the Puranas. Sage Durvasa met an apsara (celestial nymph) who gave him a garland that he, in turn, put over the head of Airavata, the elephant belonging to Indra, king of the devas. But the elephant threw it on the ground. Slighted, Durvasa cursed Indra that his kingdom and powers would be destroyed.

As their powers waned and they stood to lose their authority, the devas were afraid that the forces of evil, the asuras, would overpower them. So they rushed in panic to Brahma, the Creator, who advised them to seek out the Preserver, Vishnu. Vishnu instructed them to collect all the plants and herbs and cast them into the ocean of milk. Then, using Mount Mandara as a churning stick and the giant snake Vasuki as a rope, they must churn the ocean along with the asuras, with whom they should unite in peace. The churning would bring forth amrita, the nectar of immortality, that would restore their powers. The devas and the asuras did as they were told. But the mountain, being large and heavy, began to sink. So Vishnu incarnated himself as a gigantic tortoise, the colossus Kurma, and bore the great mountain on his back.

The churning of the ocean brought forth many wonderful things: Surabhi, the sacred cow; Varuni, goddess of wine; Parijata, the tree of paradise; the apsaras, celestial nymphs; Chandra, the cool-rayed moon; and visha, poison, claimed by the snake gods. Finally, seated on a lotus, came Lakshmi, the goddess of prosperity and the very epitome of beauty. With her came Dhanvantari, the physician of the gods, holding the immortal nectar, amrita, in a cup.

Both the devas and asuras were supposed to share the amrita. But, seeing the devas distracted by the appearance of Lakshmi, the asuras tried to steal the nectar. Immediately, Vishnu took the form of a beautiful woman, Mohini, distracted the asuras, and took away the nectar of immortality, which he gave to the devas, thereby restoring their powers.

As in the case of Matsya, the tortoise first appears in the Shatapatha Brahmana as a form of Brahma, to create offspring.

Shrikurmam in Andhra Pradesh is the only extant Kurma kshetra, or temple of Kurma. Situated between the Vamsadhara and Langali rivers, it was originally a shrine for Shiva, and was later converted to a Vaishnava temple by the medieval preacher Ramanuja. Inside the sanctum, apart from the main image of Vishnu, the first icon to greet the visitor is a tortoise with an upraised tail, its back towards the worshipper. According to a local legend, a devout Bhil king regularly worshipped the image from behind the back wall of the shrine. Pleased at his piety, Kurma turned around and faced the king. It is likely that this story was created to explain why the tortoise faces west, because this is at variance with the scriptural requirement that the main deity should face east. It is also probably an instance of a non-Vedic local tortoise god of the Bhils being integrated into the Hindu pantheon by its identification with the story of Kurma.

The samudra manthana story is extremely popular in South-east Asia, where it is found in many temples in Indonesia and Cambodia. On the walls of Angkor Wat, Vishnu dances on the back of the tortoise, while the devas and asuras hold either end of Vasuki. But the most remarkable sculptures are to be seen in the ancient Cambodian city of Angkor Thom. The entrance to the city is made up of five gigantic gates, each representing Mount Meru. Each gate is mounted by four huge heads, each head facing a cardinal direction. Each deva and asura is a larger-than-life figure.

In Khmer iconography, the earth below symbolizes the tortoise, a partial incarnation of Vishnu, whose spouse is Mother Earth. The four heads which crown the peak of Meru represent the all-seeing Vishnu. He is depicted as multi-headed on the walls of the Bayon central temple of Angkor Thom, where the story is narrated in several sequences. Vishnu's ascent to the top of the churning rod is the representation of the supreme position of the midday sun, as it traverses the skies.

Kurma avatara is generally portrayed as a four-armed figure, with the upper torso of a man and the lower torso of a tortoise.

Varaha, the Boar

The boar represents the next step in evolution, a land animal and a mammal.

The Taittiriya Aranyaka and Shatapatha Brahmana tell us that the universe was formerly water, while the earth was the size of a hand span. Becoming a boar, Prajapati (Brahma) lifted it out of the water. The Brahmana gives the boar a name, Emusha. He was also the husband of the earth. But the *Ramayana* and Vishnu Purana substitute Vishnu for Brahma when they describe the boar incarnation.

Kashyapa, a Vedic sage, married Aditi, Diti and the other daughters of Daksha, the Creative Power. Aditi gave birth to the celestial beings, the Adityas, while Diti gave birth to the demons, Daityas, including the terrible, Hiranyaksha and Hiranyakashipu. In a former birth the two were the doorkeepers of Vishnu's palace. But their arrogance had angered some sages who cursed them to be reborn as demons. They were incarnations of cruelty and caused great suffering to the people. Even the devas were harassed by them. Then, one day, the elder brother Hiranyaksha rolled Mother Earth up in a mat and threw her into the ocean. She let out a heart-rending cry that was heard as far as Vaikuntha. Immediately, Vishnu took the form of a gigantic boar and dove into the waters. There, he encountered Hiranyaksha and a terrible battle took place, in which the demon was killed. Vishnu then carried Mother Earth, cradled in his massive tusks, out

of the depths. The devas and the sages sang in praise of
the great boar. Varaha placed the earth on the ocean,
where she floats like a ship and because of her massive
expanse, does not sink beneath the waters.

The Puranas tell us that the boar was ten yojanas in
breadth and a thousand in height. He was the colour of a
dark cloud, his tusks were white, sharp and frightening.
He was as large as a mountain, with huge shoulders
and loins, and a roar that resounded like thunder. Fire
flashed from his eyes, he was as radiant as the sun and
strode like a lion. A veritable picture of majestic beauty!

The extrication of the earth from the waters also
symbolizes the saving of the earth from the deluge of sin
in which it was engulfed.

The boar incarnation appears in several inscriptions
and sculptures of the Gupta period. The most impressive
sculpture is that found in the fifth century Gupta cave at
Udayagiri in Madhya Pradesh. With a small Mother
Earth seated on his massive tusks, the gigantic Varaha
is indeed magnificent.

The town of Jhansi in Uttar Pradesh also has a famous
Varaha temple, which is now in ruins.

But the most famous home of Varaha is the temple
town of Tirumala, above Tirupati, also known as Varaha
kshetra. At the end of the Krita yuga, Varaha was asked
by his devotees to stay on earth and protect them. He
agreed and sent for his divine garden Kridachala, which

was brought from Vaikuntha by his mount Garuda and placed on the Venkata hills.And there he resides, with Vishnu's other manifestation, Venkateshwara. In fact, it is Varaha who receives the first pooja and naivedya in Tirumala.

A little-known fact is that the period we live in at present is the shweta varaha kalpa (the age of the white boar). During the sankalpa, before performing a religious ceremony, the yajamana (performer of the ritual) recites the day, date, month and period, the last being shweta varaha kalpa. It is the same white boar that is believed to reside on the hill of Tirumala.

Another important Varaha temple is to be found at Shrimushnam near Chidambaram in Tamil Nadu, where Varaha is revered equally by Hindus and Muslims. In the Tamil month of Masi (February-March), both communities take the bronze utsava murti in a grand procession to Killaiamballi village for a bath in the sea, as a re-enactment of Varaha's feat. The deity in this temple is credited with so many miracles that the name Varaha Saheb is common even among Muslims in this area.

While the fish and tortoise are represented with the animal forming the lower torso and the man the upper, it is the reverse in the case of Varaha. He is always a boar-headed man, with his four arms holding the attributes of Vishnu.

There is a myth that tells of Varaha and the Earth having a child, Naraka, out of wedlock, whose paternity is hidden from Vishnu by his mother. Naraka is an asura, the rich and powerful ruler of Patala or the netherworld, who is later killed by Vishnu. His paternity is revealed only at the time of his death. Naraka is a Hindu Lord of Hades, a result of being hidden away from the world above. In South Indian tradition, he was killed by Krishna on Deepavali, which is also called Naraka Chaturdashi and is the annual celebration of Vishnu's destruction of the forces of evil.

In Indian tradition, the boar is closely associated with water and believed to be able to predict the coming of the rains. Its ability to lift the earth with its tusks probably linked it with the tilling and ploughing of the soil, an agricultural activity. The story of Varaha is thus the story of the rescue of the earth from the all-consuming waters. Naraka, son of the boar and the earth, is identified with the Rig Vedic demon of drought, Vritra. As the boar ploughs and saves the earth, Vishnu conquers drought. It is a triumph of agriculture and man's ability to produce food. Deepavali comes during the monsoon season (November) in the south and is a celebration of rain conquering drought and saving the earth and the crops.

Narasimha, the Man-Lion

After Hiranyaksha was killed, his brother Hiranyakashipu swore to avenge his death. Although he was as evil as his brother, he underwent extreme austerities and received a powerful boon from Brahma. He would not die at the hands of either man or animal, not at night nor in the day, neither in the house nor outside, not on earth nor in the sky nor under water, with neither a weapon, nor fire, nor water. This unique boon made Hiranyakashipu savage and cruel. He denied the existence of the gods and took over the earth, the heavens and the nether world. He was inflated with pride and ruled the world with terror and fear.

Hiranyakashipu had a son, Prahlada, who was a devout worshipper of Vishnu. Whenever he was asked by his father to repeat what he had studied, Prahlada would sing the praises of Vishnu. This made Hiranyakashipu furious and he began to hate his son. He threatened to have him killed, but this did not deter Prahlada from his faith. Consumed by hatred, Hiranyakashipu ordered his demon hordes to attack Prahlada with their weapons, but the prince was not afraid of them.

Then Hiranyakashipu commanded the snakes to bite Prahlada to death. They bit till their fangs were broken and their jewelled crests burst, till there was fever in their hoods and fear in their heart. But young Prahlada remained unscathed. Hiranyakashipu then ordered elephants to throw down his son and trample him. But Prahlada continued to meditate on Vishnu and the elephants' tusks were blunted against his breast. A heap of wood was piled around the prince and lit, in order to burn him to death. But it felt cool and fragrant against Prahlada's skin. The prince was then administered poison. But this too proved futile. Hiranyakashipu hurled him, bound, into the depths of the ocean. But Prahlada thought of Vishnu and was saved each time.

Fed up, Hiranyakashipu asked him where he could see this Vishnu. To Prahlada's reply 'everywhere', the king kicked a pillar and asked him if the god lived in the pillar. Out sprang Narasimha from the pillar. He had a lion's head with a man's body—neither man nor animal. He fought the wicked demon and dragged him to the doorway—neither inside the house nor outside. It was sunset—neither night nor day. And then Narasimha, the man-lion incarnation of Vishnu, killed Hiranyakashipu by tearing his body with his claws—using neither sword nor fire nor water. Thus, Vishnu killed the evil demon without violating Brahma's boon.

It is said that so crazed was Narasimha at the sight of blood that the lion in him became uncontrollable and went on a terrorizing spree. The devas, even Brahma and Shiva, were unable to stop him. It was left to Vishnu's devotee Prahlada to finally calm the lion in the god and restore him to a state of tranquillity.

This is the first instance of an incarnation accompanied by an ardent devotee. The two are Narayana and Nara, one acting, the other worshipping.

The cult of Narasimha is extremely popular in Andhra Pradesh, Karnataka and northern Tamil Nadu where thousands of Narasimha temples, both big and small, are found. There are, in particular, thirty-two Narasimha temples in Andhra Pradesh that are important pilgrimage centres.

The most important is the temple of Roudra (angry) Narasimha at Ahobalam in Andhra Pradesh. This is believed to be the spot where Narasimha killed Hiranyakashipu. The pillar from which Narasimha emerged and the lake where he washed his blood-stained hands are situated here. So important is this shrine that the seat of the Vadagalai (northern branch) sect of Vaishnavism is situated at Ahobalam and the head of the sect is known as Alagiya Singar (the beautiful lion).

The most famous temple of Narasimha is located on the hill of Simhachalam, near the coastal city and port of Vishakhapatnam in Andhra Pradesh. The deity is known as Varahanarasimhamurti and is smeared with sandalwood paste to cool his anger after the killing of the demon. Simhachalam's importance grew from the fact that Prahlada was believed to have lived and ruled here.

Other important Narasimha temples in Andhra

Pradesh include those at:

- Antarvedi where, it is believed, Hiranyakashipu's corpse fell when it was thrown into the air by Narasimha;
- Khaadri, where the terrifying aspect of Ugra (angry) Narasimha settled down;
- Anatavadi, believed to be a replica of a Narasimha temple constructed by the five Pandava brothers of the *Mahabharata*;
- Mangalagiri, believed to have been constructed by the eldest Pandava Yudhishthira;
- Penna Ahobalam, on the river Penna, where there is no icon, and only the footprints of Narasimha, measuring five feet by three, are visible for worship;
- Khamam, built by the Kakatiya rulers;
- Korukunda, built by the Chalukya kings;
- Singapatnam, where Narasimha is in the form of Shiva's Linga;
- Kondurg, where the image is in a cave in a hill, which has neither steps nor passage for ascent;
- Singarayakonda, the hill of 'King Lion' or Singaraya.

Namakkal in Tamil Nadu is home to a well-known Narasimha temple.

Holenarasipur, Saligrama, Konnakuntla and Karpara Kshetra are some of the important sites in Karnataka, although the most impressive is the massive

Narasimha image at Hampi, the former capital of the Vijayanagara empire. Hewn out of a single boulder in AD 1528, during the reign of King Krishnadevaraya, the details of the figure and its ornamentation have been finished in intricate detail. On the base of the pedestal are carved the sun and the moon, testifying that the image will last forever. In spite of the broken parts, the twenty-two feet high colossus is an awe-inspiring and majestic figure.

Other important temples are those of Ugra Narasimha at Joshimath, Uttar Pradesh and Vidal Nrusingha Mandir at Nrusinghanath, Orissa, and the ones at Rather and Charthana in Maharashtra.

Narasimha is portrayed as a lion-headed man. Sometimes Lakshmi is seated on his knee, and this form is known as Lakshmi Narasimha.

The proliferation of the cult and the association of the story with several sites in Andhra Pradesh suggest that Narasimha was a popular local deity. Prahlada is believed to have been the ruler of Simhachalam and it is likely that the cult of his god Narasimha originated here.

Narasimha represents the beginning of the evolution of *Homo sapiens*, the transition from a four-legged species to man.

Vamana, the Dwarf

Vishnu's incarnation Vamana resonates with the Rig Vedic description of the solar deity who takes three strides across the skies.

Bali, son of Virochana and grandson of Prahlada, and therefore belonging to the Asura lineage, conquered Indra, king of the gods, and assumed the kingship of the universe. The gods were forced to leave Indra's heaven Amaravati.

To celebrate his victory, Bali conducted an elaborate sacrifice. Distraught, Indra and the other gods went to Vishnu for help. They asked him to take advantage of Bali's famed generosity and request the demon to restore the kingship of the worlds to Indra. For Bali was known to never refuse a supplicant.

Vishnu agreed to help the gods defeat Bali and regain the heavens. He then took birth as a dwarf, the son of sage Kashyapa and Aditi. He visited Bali's sacrifice in Indra's heaven. Bali was so impressed by the radiance of the young boy's face that he offered to give him whatever he wished—gold, houses, villages, food, drink, horses, elephants, cows and carriages. Vamana replied that a wise man should ask for no more than his needs, and all that he required was a small portion of ground, as covered by 'three paces measured step by step'. Bali's preceptor Shukracharya, the teacher of the demons, recognised Vishnu and advised Bali to refuse. But Bali insisted on fulfilling his promise, saying that he would rather lose his home than break his word.

So Vishnu took his three steps. With the first he covered the earth. With the second, the sky and the heavens. Then he reproached Bali for not providing him a place for the third step and condemned him to the nether world. Bali, who did not fear hell as much as he feared a bad name, offered his own head as a resting-place for the third step.

Vishnu placed his foot on Bali's head and started crushing him. But Prahlada appeared and pleaded with Vamana to spare his grandson, for he did not deserve the punishment. Vishnu relented and pressed down upon Bali till the latter went down to Patala, the nether world.

The germ of this story is to be found in the Shatapatha Brahmana. The asuras had won the earth and decided to divide it among themselves. The gods heard of this and wanted to regain the earth. They placed Vishnu at the head of the sacrifice and asked for a share of the earth. As Vishnu had taken the form of a dwarf (in this story), the asuras offered as much land as he could lie on. The gods accepted and thus acquired the whole earth.

In contemporary Kerala, the people believe that Bali was an ancient ruler of their land. After Bali had been defeated by Vishnu as Vamana, his subjects were miserable at his impending departure and begged him not to leave. Bali requested Vishnu for permission to visit his people once a year. Vishnu granted him his wish. Bali's yearly visit to his kingdom is celebrated in Kerala as the annual harvest festival of Onam, in the month of Chingom. It is likely that this story is an allegorical representation of the coming of the harvest and the offering of thanksgiving (bali) after a hot dry summer (the solar Vishnu).

Mavelikara in Kerala is the site of a famous temple of Vamana, locally known as Thrikkakarai. It is believed that Vishnu pressed King Bali into the earth here.

Vamana may be represented either as a dwarf or a giant with his foot on the head of a crouching Bali. A massive Trivikrama lifting one leg is sculpted in the early Chalukya cave temple of Badami in Karnataka.

A huge Vamana as the giant Trivikrama is the chief deity of the temple of Ulagalanda Perumal (Vishnu who measured the world) at Kanchipuram.

On the evolutionary scale, Vamana is an imperfect specimen, a dwarf. He thus represents the earliest *Homo sapiens,* who were quite small, as palaeontology has discovered.

Parashurama, Rama with the Axe

Vishnu incarnated himself as Parashurama to destroy the Kshatriyas, the warrior caste, who had become very arrogant and were constantly at war.

Parashurama, or Rama with the axe, was the fifth son of the sage Jamadagni and Renuka, and was also known as Rama Jamadagnya.

Renuka was a pious women, known for her dutifulness and abilities as a good housewife. One day, as she went to bathe in the river, she saw Chitraratha, prince of Mrittikavati, sporting with his wife in the water. She felt envious of their fun and frolic and returned to her hermitage in a state of disquiet. Her perspicacious husband immediately sensed her mood and realised that she had lost her perfection and sanctity. Furious, he sent for his sons and demanded that they kill their mother. The first four refused, and were cursed by their father to become idiots.

Then Parashurama appeared. When confronted with his father's order, the dutiful son immediately picked up his axe and cut off Renuka's head. Pleased, Jamadagni offered Parashurama whatever he desired. The latter immediately asked that his mother be brought back to life with no memory of her death, her purification from all defilement and the restoration of his brothers to sanity. He also asked for invincibility in single combat and a long life for himself. Jamadagni acceded to all his wishes.

Now King Kaartavirya of the Haihaya tribe had

been endowed with a thousand arms and a golden chariot that took him where he willed. But he was a wicked oppressor of the gods, sages and people. One day, he came to the hermitage of Jamadagni. In her husband's absence, Renuka received him with courtesy and respect. Instead of acknowledging her hospitality, the arrogant king took away the calf of her milch cow. When Parashurama returned home he saw the cow in great distress. On hearing the story, he challenged Kaartavirya to battle. He destroyed the thousand arms of the king and killed him.

To avenge their father's death, the sons of Kaartavirya visited the hermitage during Parashurama's absence and killed the aged and unresisting sage Jamadagni. When Parashurama returned and saw his father's murdered body, he was furious. He vowed to wipe out the race of Kshatriyas from the face of the earth. He pursued this mission with zeal stopping only when all Kshatriyas, including children, were destroyed.

While this story is common to the epics and the Puranas, the *Ramayana* continues the tale to tell us that Rama, prince of Ayodhya and the next incarnation of Vishnu, finally curbed Parashurama.

Rama was returning to his kingdom Ayodhya after breaking Shiva's mighty bow at the court of Janaka in Mithila, thereby acquiring the hand of Janaka's daughter Sita. Parashurama accosted him, since Rama was a

Kshatriya prince and Parashurama had sworn to kill all Kshatriyas. Parashurama challenged Rama to bend the bow of Vishnu. Rama accepted the challenge and strung and bent the huge bow. Rama refused to kill Parashurama as he was a Brahmin, but destroyed all the wonderful abodes created by him. Parashurama was forced to go away and live out the rest of his days in the Himalayas.

It is commonly believed that this story is an interpolation in the *Ramayana* to acknowledge the divinity of Rama and his identification with Vishnu.

The worship of Parashurama is mentioned in a north Indian epigraph dated AD 200. The south-west coast of India—Goa, southern coastal Karnataka and Kerala— is known as Parashurama kshetra and is believed to have been retrieved from the sea by Parashurama. As he had killed numerous men, Parashurama had to undergo punishment and went on a pilgrimage doing useful things, one of which was the reclamation of the west coast. According to one story, it was a gift from Varuna, lord of the seas, after Parashurama shot an arrow into the water to drive back the sea. Another version says that he drove back the sea and cut fissures in the mountains (Western Ghats). He is said to have brought Brahmins from the north to this region, and the Namboodri Brahmins of Kerala claim to have come south with Parashurama. He is also credited with the construction of thousands of temples and the establishment of rituals based on the Sanskrit scriptures in this region.

The hermitage of Jamadagni, where Parashurama cut off his mother's head, is believed to have been situated in the village of Renuka near Nahan in Himachal Pradesh. The Parashurama temple is situated on the banks of the Parashuram Tal (lake). It is a popular site of pilgrimage and is locally known as Purani Deoti (ancient goddess).

Renuka Devi is also a popular village goddess of south India. She is represented by the headless figure of a woman with a pot in lieu of her head.

At Trichur in Kerala, the Vadakkunathan (northern lord) temple enshrines a small sacred dais called the Shri Moolasthanam, built in memory of Parashurama. It is said that before he disappeared, Parashurama gave his final instructions to the local Namboodri priests from this spot. He also promised to come back whenever they needed him and taught them some chants and rituals with which to call upon him. All was well for many years till a few young sceptics decided to test the efficacy of his instructions. Parashurama appeared on the dais, furious. Cursing them, he disappeared, vowing never to return.

The Parashurama Devalaya at Nanjangud in Karnataka and the Parashurameshwar Mandir at Bhubaneshwar in Orissa are other important temples.

The Parashurama temple at Phede in Maharashtra has a very interesting story associated with it. A wealthy Muslim lady belonging to the Adil Shahi dynasty of Bijapur dispatched her ships filled with merchandise to Arabia. A terrible storm arose over the Arabian Sea. Fearful for the safety of her ships, she prayed to Lord Parashurama, for if he could subdue the seas and reclaim the land he could surely save her ships. Immediately, the storm subsided and the ships reached their destination safely. She built a temple in his honour in the village of Phede, which became a major pilgrimage center for Hindus and Muslims.

Parashurama is generally described and portrayed as angry, hotheaded and uncontrollable. He is reminiscent of popular stories of the Stone Age man. Interestingly, even his battles were fought one-to-one, an axe in his hand.

Rama, the Perfect Man

The story of Rama, written by the sage Valmiki, is the basis for the *Ramayana*, one of India's two great Sanskrit epics. The persona of Rama is a role model for all Indians and the story is popular in every nook and corner of the country. It has been retold in every Indian language and has travelled as far as East and South-east Asia.

Although the story of Rama has been narrated in every Indian and South-east Asian language, Valmiki's *Ramayana* is the oldest and the most authentic.

Rama was the prince of Ayodhya, born to destroy the wicked demons, particularly Ravana, who were terrorizing the earth and preventing the sages from completing their ritual sacrifices. To help him, the Earth incarnated herself as Sita, daughter of Janaka of Mithila, and the serpent Adi Shesha was born as Lakshmana, his brother and constant companion. The story is long but fairly straightforward.

Dasharatha was the king of Ayodhya in northern India. Childless, he performed the Ashvamedha or horse sacrifice. Pleased with his devotion, Agni, the God of Fire, appeared before the king and gave him a gruel that his three wives were to drink to beget children. In time, his first wife Kaushalya produced Rama, the eldest son, his second wife Kaikeyi produced Bharata and his third wife Sumitra produced twins, Lakshmana and Shatrughna. There was great rejoicing in the kingdom upon the birth of an heir. Rama's birth is still celebrated on the ninth day after the full moon in the month of Chaitra (March-April) every year as Ramanavami.

When Rama was sixteen, the sage Vishwamitra came to Dasharatha's court and asked for his sons' help in vanquishing two rakshasas or demons—Marichi and Subahu—who were preventing the conduct of his sacrifices. Dasharatha reluctantly let his boys go. While they battled the demons, Vishwamitra taught them many spells and the use of arms. And when they finally killed the rakshasas, Vishwamitra took them to the court of king Janaka of Mithila to bend the untamed bow of Shiva. On the way Rama released Ahalya, wife of the sage Gautama, from her curse. Long ago, Ahalya had had an adulterous relationship with Indra, who had come to her disguised as her husband. When the sage found out, he cursed her to spend aeons as a stone, till Rama appeared and liberated her.

Janaka had organized a competition for the hand of his beautiful daughter Sita, found as a baby in a furrow as Janaka ploughed the land. He declared that only he who could bend the mighty bow of Shiva would be worthy of his lovely daughter. None of the assembled kings were able to lift the bow, leave alone bend it. Rama tried and succeeded, winning the hand of the much sought-after princess. A message was dispatched to Dasharatha, who arrived with his queens. Apart from the marriage of

Rama and Sita, Rama's three brothers were married to three other daughters of Janaka.

Upon their return to Ayodhya, Dasharatha desired to abdicate in favour of his eldest son, Rama. His second wife Kaikeyi, egged on by her maidservant Manthara, was very upset by her husband's decision. Manthara reminded her queen of a promise of two boons made by the king long ago, after she had nursed him back to health from a battle injury. Kaikeyi demanded that the boons be granted, and asked for the kingdom for her son Bharata, and Rama to be banished to the forest. The king begged, pleaded and demanded, but Kaikeyi stood firm. Finally Rama, when told of the promise, insisted it should be honoured. He left for the forest with his favourite brother Lakshmana and his wife Sita, both of whom insisted on accompanying him.

They reached the Dandaka forest and settled at Chitrakoot. Meanwhile, bereft of his eldest and favourite son, Dasharatha died of a broken heart, necessitating the return of Kaikeyi's son, Bharata, who had been away and was unaware of Rama's banishment. Bharata refused to ascend the throne and went in search of Rama, to bring him back. But the elder brother insisted on fulfilling his father's promise. Finally, Bharata took Rama's slippers to place upon the throne, agreeing to rule as regent till his brother's return after fourteen years. To expiate for his mother's sin, Bharata lived out the period as an ascetic outside the city.

Rama, Lakshmana and Sita had several adventures in the forest and killed many demons. The story of their travels is a geographical record of the Indian heartland. After ten years they reached the hermitage of Agastya on the banks of the river Godavari.

One day, Shurpanakha, sister of Ravana, the demon king of Lanka (Sri Lanka), passed by and seeing the handsome Rama, fell madly in love with him. She asked him to marry her but he refused, pointing out that he already had a wife. Then she asked Lakshmana, but he too refused. Deciding that Sita was the obstacle to her marriage, she attacked Sita. Lakshmana jumped to Sita's rescue and cut off Shurpanakha's nose and ears. Furious, she went to her brother Ravana and narrated the incident. Knowing her brother's weakness for beautiful women, she praised Sita's beauty till Ravana decided he had to have Sita. He told his minister Maricha to assume the form of a golden deer and distract Sita. Maricha tried to dissuade Ravana, but to no avail.

So Maricha went to the hermitage in the form of a spotted deer. Sita immediately desired the beautiful creature, and Rama went in chase, commanding Lakshmana to watch over Sita. But as the deer kept disappearing and reappearing, Rama realized it was a demon, and shot at it with his bow and arrow. As the demon-deer breathed his last he called out for Sita and Lakshmana.

Assuming that Rama was injured, Sita begged Lakshmana to go in search of his brother. Lakshmana drew a line in front of their hut and advised her not to step out of it while he went to seek Rama. The term 'Lakshman rekha' (Lakshmana's line) has, in Indian culture, become a synonym for the boundaries of behaviour and decorum.

As soon as Lakshmana left, Ravana appeared in the form of a holy mendicant. He persuaded Sita to step beyond the line and give him food. As soon as she crossed the line, he forcibly dragged her into his magical chariot and flew off with her to Lanka. There he housed her in a grove of ashoka trees guarded by female demons and harassed her night and day to marry him. The virtuous Sita naturally refused.

Meanwhile, Rama and Lakshmana returned and discovered Sita's abduction. Crazed with grief, they went in search of her. They traced Ravana's journey by signs they found along the way. The first was the dying vulture Jatayu, who had fought Ravana while trying to save Sita. Then they came upon the Vanara (monkey) tribe whose exiled king Sugriva had saved Sita's jewels as she had thrown them down from the sky as signposts for Rama to find her. Rama killed Sugriva's brother Vali, thereby enabling Sugriva to regain his position and his

wife Tara. While Rama was with the Vanaras, one of
their tribesmen, Hanuman, became his ardent devotee.
And it was he who flew to Sri Lanka to discover the
whereabouts of Sita. The Vanaras then helped Rama
build a bridge across the sea near Rameshwaram, in
order to cross over to Lanka. A fierce battle ensued in
which all the demons—including, finally, Ravana—were
killed and Sita was rescued. Sita was then called upon
to prove her chastity, which she did by entering the fire.
Finally, the gods descended to vouch for her purity and
Rama took her back.

The brothers and Sita returned to Ayodhya with their
Vanara friends just in time to prevent Bharata from
entering the fire, as the fourteen years of exile were over.
Rama was crowned king and ruled justly and wisely for
many years, ushering in a period of peace and prosperity.
In popular tradition, his reign was the golden age of
Indian history, or Ram Rajya.

A later interpolation in the *Ramayana*, the Uttara
Khanda, has Rama banishing Sita from the palace
because of the doubts of a washerman. She goes to the
hermitage of the sage Valmiki where she gives birth to
twin sons. She later sends the twins to their father's court
to reclaim their heritage. Rama asks her to assert her
innocence and return, but this is too much for Sita. She
asks Mother Earth, who gave birth to her, to take her
back. The earth opens up and swallows her. Rama then

loses interest in life. Going to the banks of the river Ganga he leaves his body and ascends to his heavenly home. But there is no authentication for the Uttara Khanda, which was probably added much later when women were socially repressed.

Rama is, to Hindus, the embodiment of perfection. He is the perfect son and husband, the ideal ruler and, most important, the perfect man. Similarly, Sita is the perfect woman and wife, Hanuman the perfect devotee and Lakshmana and Bharata the perfect brothers. The *Ramayana* thus symbolizes the value systems of Hindu society.

Some scholars have seen, in the Rama-Ravana conflict, the clash between the Aryans and the non-Aryans. While many stories of the killing of rakshasas seem to confirm this theory, there is strong evidence to the contrary. Firstly, the *Ramayana* was written by Valmiki, a low-caste thief turned sage. It is highly unlikely that he was part of the ruling Aryan establishment. If Rama were decimating the tribals, Valmiki would not have made him the hero of his epic. Secondly, Ravana, king of the rakshasas, was a Brahmin, while Rama was a Kshatriya. So the Aryan-non Aryan confrontation is ruled out. Finally, Rama's allies, the Vanaras, were obviously a totemic non-Aryan tribe.

How true is the story of the *Ramayana*? With the limited archaeological evidence, it is not possible to answer the question. But the *Ramayana* is a book of geographical exactitude, with correct routes and accurate descriptions of local geological formations, whether it is the description of the bend in the river Narmada at Nasik or the height of the hill in Rameshwaram. It is highly unlikely that Valmiki the writer would have travelled the country to collect this information. Obviously, the knowledge was already available.

Also, Valmiki's Rama was human, not divine. The identification came later—Kalidasa's *Raghuvamsha* (AD 400) and a Vakataka inscription of the fifth century identify Rama with Vishnu.

Thus, it appears likely that a king called Rama did live around 1000 BC. The story is so geographically accurate, and so many places all over the country are associated with Rama, that it could not have been a creation of the imagination.

Rama travelled from Ayodhya in Uttar Pradesh to Rameshwaram in southern Tamil Nadu, so sacred places connected with him are found all over the country. The most important sites connected with Rama are situated in Uttar Pradesh, where he lived and reigned. Ayodhya, where he was born; Benares, where his devotee Tulsidas lived and composed the *Ramcharitmanas*; and Rishikesh, where a temple enshrines Rama's brother Bharata, are some of the major sites. Rama, Lakshmana and Sita lived for a while at the site of the Rama temple at Ramtek in Madhya Pradesh, while the Sitarama temple at Ahairi in West Bengal celebrates the release of Ahalya from her curse. Nasik on the Narmada river in Maharashtra, and Bhadrachalam and Parnashala on the Godavari river in Andhra Pradesh are other places that Rama visited. He met Sugriva and Hanuman near Hampi, the ancient capital of Vijayanagara in Karnataka. He received and crowned Vibheeshana, Ravana's brother who changed sides, and worshipped the Shiva linga prior to the war in the pilgrimage town of Rameshwaram in Tamil Nadu. His footprints are enshrined here, on the Gandamadana Parvata hill from where Hanuman started on his journey to Lanka.

These are just a few places connected with the story of Rama. There are many more, and an infinite number of temples—big and small—all over the country which celebrate this incarnation of Vishnu.

Rama is represented in many forms. He may be the ascetic with his bow and arrow, flanked by Lakshmana, Sita and Hanuman. This form is known as Kodanda Rama. Or he may be depicted seated on his throne, generally at his coronation, the beginning of Ram Rajya, a period of prosperity. This form is known as Pattabhi Rama (from pattabhishekha or coronation).

The *Ramayana* has been translated into every Indian language and the story of Rama is so embedded in the lives of the common people that his name is invoked at every instance, sung at prayer meetings and chanted during meditation. Even at the time of death, the body is taken to the crematorium and assigned to the flames to the accompaniment of Rama's name. For it is believed that when he left the earth, Rama took all the inhabitants of Ayodhya to Brahma's heaven, without them suffering death.

Krishna, the Philosopher King

If the *Ramayana* provides the goal of perfection, the *Mahabharata*, the other great epic, is the story of imperfect people and situations, and how Vishnu, as the incarnation Krishna, manages these contradictions. The story of Krishna has to be sifted out of the story of the enmity between two sets of brothers belonging to the Kuru family. But the *Mahabharata* is of enormous proportions. Several sub-plots and unconnected stories divert from the main epic. The story of each incarnation of Vishnu runs into several chapters. In fact, later texts such as the Vishnu Purana, Bhagavata Purana and the *Harivamsha* focus far more on Krishna, although the *Mahabharata* is the oldest and most authentic source. The *Mahabharata* vacillates between treating Krishna as a hero and as a god. In Puranic literature he is always a god.

If the story of Rama was long but straightforward, the story of Krishna is longer and meanders. The tale begins with Ugrasena, king of Mathura, who was childless. One day, when his beautiful wife was walking alone in a wood, a demon became so enamoured of her that he assumed the form of her husband. The result of their union was the demon Kamsa, an incarnation of the demon Kalanemi, son of Virochana and grandson of Hiranyakashipu (of the Narasimha avatara story). Kamsa had a wicked and cruel disposition. The earth groaned under the burden of his evil actions. He deposed his father and assumed the throne, proclaiming himself king and god.

Greatly worried by Kamsa's malevolent powers, the gods went to Brahma who directed them to Vishnu, who agreed to incarnate himself on earth as Krishna, son of Kamsa's sister Devaki, with his faithful companion Adi Shesha as his brother Balarama.

Now, Ugrasena's brother Devaka had a sweet-natured daughter Devaki, who was given in marriage to Vasudeva of the Yadava race. Vasudeva was also the brother of Kunti, mother of the Pandavas.

As the marriage party was leaving, with Kamsa himself driving his sister's chariot, a voice called out from the skies that the eighth child of Devaki would be his killer. Kamsa went to kill his sister, but Vasudeva offered to give him all their children if he spared her life. So Kamsa imprisoned Devaki and Vasudeva and had them guarded night and day. Six children were born to them, and all were slaughtered. The seventh child was the incarnation of Adi Shesha. He was transferred to the womb of Rohini, another wife of Vasudeva who lived in Gokul, and was born as Balarama. Kamsa was informed that Devaki had miscarried.

The birth of Krishna took place late at night on the eighth day of the second fortnight in the month of Shravan or Bhadrapada (July-August), celebrated annually as Krishna Janmashtami. The guards fell asleep and the gates opened. A voice commanded Vasudeva to take the child to the home of Nanda the cowherd and exchange the baby for the daughter just born to Yashoda, Nanda's wife. Vasudeva crossed the river Yamuna, exchanged the children and returned to the prison. The next morning Kamsa arrived and dashed the baby against a stone. But the child was Nidra (sleep) who rose into the sky and informed Kamsa that his destroyer was born and lived elsewhere. The enraged Kamsa went on a rampage, killing every new-born child in the region. Fearful for the safety of his child, Nanda took the baby away to Gokul where Krishna and Balarama grew up as brothers.

The story of Krishna's childhood is a combination of mythical exploits and childhood pranks and has created an entire literature and cult around Krishna. From babyhood to adulthood he is credited with the destruction of many demons sent by Kamsa to kill him, and with the release of heavenly beings cursed to live on earth: Putana the female demon was killed by baby Krishna, and the sons of Kubera the god of wealth were liberated by him from their curse. Other demons destroyed by him include the whirlwind demon Trinavartta, the crane demon Bakasura, the horse demon Hayas and the bull demon Arishta. All these adventures took place on the banks of the Yamuna. But the river itself was poisoned by the many-headed snake Kaliya.

One day, when Krishna was playing with his friends, his ball fell into the river. Kaliya caught him in his coils, but Krishna expanded in size till Kaliya let go. Then Krishna danced on the snake, nearly killing him in the process, till the many wives of Kaliya begged for their husband's life. Krishna banished Kaliya to Ramanaka Dvipa (in the Bay of Bengal) and the waters of the Yamuna became fit for bathing and drinking.

Krishna also took on Indra himself. He advised the cowherds to worship the mountain Govardhana in Brindavan, for the mountain was the source of their prosperity. An angry Indra attacked them with thunder and rain, but Krishna lifted the mountain itself to save his people. Indra conceded defeat and offered homage to Krishna. This story probably indicates the shifting of popular worship from Indra to Krishna.

There are also many stories of the pranks he played on his mother and the gopis, or cowherdesses, with whom he loved to dance. Much later, these tales formed the basis of a whole cult of Krishna and Radha, his favourite gopi. But this was a development of the medieval period. In early literature, he was married to Satyabhama, daughter of Satyajit; later, after he moved to Dwarka he married Rukmini, daughter of Bhishmaka, king of Vidarbha, as well as other princesses.

Unsuccessful in his attempts to kill Krishna, Kamsa invited the brothers to the annual athletic events at

Mathura. On their way, they were attacked by the horse demon Kesin whom they destroyed. At the games, two wrestlers, with orders to kill Krishna, descended on the brothers, but were killed, while an elephant sent to trample them to death was slain. Kamsa then ordered his soldiers to attack and kill Krishna and Balarama, but Krishna attacked and killed Kamsa himself. He installed Ugrasena on the throne and took up residence in Mathura along with his wife and Balarama.

Krishna was the protector of Mathura, but later moved to Dwarka on the Gujarat coast. He defeated and killed Jarasandha, Kamsa's father-in-law; Sunaman, Kamsa's brother; Kalayavana, king of the Yavanas (Persians); Naraka, king of Pragjyotisha (in Patala); Shishupala, the reincarnation of Ravana and Hiranyakashipu, Pralambha, Jambha, Pitha and Muru. He destroyed Saubha, the flying city of the demons, and decimated several tribes such as the Angas and Bangas. There is also a 'false' Vasudeva Krishna, an identity assumed by one Paundraka, who was killed by Krishna's discus.

The conch and the discus held by Vishnu are actually obtained by Krishna. By killing the demon Panchajanya, he obtained the conch, Panchajanya. By propitiating Agni, the god of fire, in the Khandva forest, he procured the chakra or discus.

Krishna's miracles are legion. When the Kauravas

seek to disrobe and humiliate Draupadi in the court of Hastinapura, he makes her sari endless. He saves the Pandavas from the house of lac set on fire by the Kauravas. In the great *Mahabharata* war, Krishna gives the two sides a choice: one would have his army, the other would have him, but he would not fight. The Kauravas choose first and take the army. The Pandavas choose second and prefer to have Krishna, who assumes the role of Arjuna's charioteer, hence the name Parthasarathi (Partha was another name for Arjuna, sarathi means chariot driver). Needless to say, the Pandavas won, but not without a terrible war of death and destruction.

At the commencement of the war, when Arjuna declares his preference for renunciation over fighting his relatives and peers, Krishna reveals the Bhagavad Gita or divine song, whereby he extols duty without thought of reward as essential for the triumph of good over evil. The Bhagavad Gita contains the essentials of Upanishadic philosophy communicated in simple language and uncluttered explanations. As he delivers his discourse, Krishna reveals his Vishwaroopa or Universal Form, whereby all creation, the stars, planets, people, animals, plants and more are found to be within Vishnu himself. And Krishna reveals that he is not merely an incarnation, he is the Supreme Being himself.

Krishna's end is foretold, as was his birth. Some

Yadava boys had, as a joke, dressed up Krishna's son Samba in women's clothes and asked the sages whether 'she' would give birth to a male or female child. The sages retorted that she would bring forth a club that would destroy the Yadava race. Accordingly, a club came out of Samba. King Ugrasena ordered that it should be crushed to a powder and thrown into the sea. But the powder fell on the shore and became rushes, while a small part of the club, which could not be broken, was thrown into the sea. This was swallowed by a fish, which was caught by a fisherman and the fragment was made into an arrowhead by a hunter named Jara.

When Krishna decided to leave the world, he thought he would save his Yadava tribesmen from the curse of total annihilation by sending them to Prabhasa. Unfortunately, they got drunk, quarrelled and killed each other with the rushes. Krishna and Balarama were unable to stop the massacre. Then a serpent crawled out of Balarama's mouth—the serpent Adi Shesha, of whom he was an incarnation—and Balarama left the earth. Krishna was sitting alone in meditation when the hunter Jara mistook him for a deer and shot at him. When Jara discovered what he had done he was horrified, but was forgiven by Krishna, who granted him instant salvation. Then Krishna abandoned his mortal body and left the earth. Dwarka was the Yadava kingdom established by Krishna. After his death it was submerged by the ocean and the Yadavas perished with it (although later royal lines and communities claim to be Yadavas). Recent excavations in the sea off Bet Dwarka have revealed a fortified city conforming to the epic descriptions of Dwarka.

If Rama is an enigma, Krishna is even more so. The sudden transition from child to warrior to Supreme God has made him the most complex deity of the pantheon. This complexity has spawned a number of theories of the origin of the god, some fantastic, others very logical. There are certain irreconcilable problems in the character of Krishna:

- The child Krishna was brought up by the tribe of Abhiras (modern-day Ahirs) and is still considered to be their god.
- After Krishna leaves Brindavan for Mathura, he never looks back. His parents are no longer described as Nanda and Yashoda. He is celebrated as the Vrishni or Yadava king of Dwarka, Vasudeva-Krishna, son of Vasudeva and Devaki. He is now a ruler and a consummate politician, and a friend of the Pandavas who he helps in the *Mahabharata* war.
- Krishna expounds his philosophy in the Bhagavad Gita. But there is an earlier Krishna Devakiputra (son of Devaki), disciple of the sage Ghora Angirasa and author of the Chandogya Upanishad. A line-by-

line comparison of the two books reveals amazing similarities.

So, who was Krishna? Were there three figures—the child god of the Abhiras, the Yadava king and the philosopher—combined into one? Or were the king Vasudeva Krishna and the philosopher of the same name one, leaving the child god of the Abhiras as a second figure? Or were all three different aspects of the same deity, as the Puranas suggest? We will never know the truth.

In the conflict with Indra and Krishna's advice to the cowherds not to worship the Vedic deity, it appears that Krishna directly challenged the supremacy of the Vedic gods, his own cult becoming superior to theirs. Krishna was a heroic figure fighting evil men and demons. It is no wonder, then, that Megasthenes, the Greek ambassador at the court of Chandragupta Maurya, called him Herakles (Hercules).

Professor H.C. Raychaudhuri has established the dates of the *Mahabharata* and Krishna from the list of dynasties in the *Mahabharata*, which corresponds to the Greek versions and the Buddhist and Jaina traditions. According to him, Krishna lived around 900 BC. The archaeological findings at Kurukshetra also corroborate this date.

In the association of Arjuna and Krishna we see a

reflection of the combination of Indra and Vishnu. One is the doer, the other the all-seeing Supreme, the duo of Nara and Narayana, as described in the *Mahabharata*. This combination is different from Rama and Lakshmana or Krishna and Balarama, where one is the god and the other is his companion Adi Shesha.

Temples to Krishna dot the whole country. But the most important are those associated with his story.

The most sacred shrine to Krishna is the Krishna Janmabhoomi temple at Mathura. It is a tiny cell beneath the ground surmounted by a huge temple complex. Near the temple is Rangabhoomi, where he is said to have killed Kamsa. A few kilometres from Mathura is Brindavan, associated with Krishna's childhood.

The tales and traditions of Krishna form an important part of the local lore and culture of Gujarat, thanks to the saint-preacher Vallabhacharya who was an ardent devotee. The main temples here are on the island of Bet Dwarka and the main Dwarkadeesh temple of Dwarka. Krishna left the earth at Veraval, having completed the task for which he was born. Although it is not connected with the story of Krishna, the temple of Shrinathji at Nathadwara is as famous as the sites of Krishna's story. The icon holds up an arm to greet his devotees. This image is believed to have been originally made at Vraja in the Himalayas.

Other important Krishna temples include Jagannatha

of Puri, an obviously tribal figure, the temples of Vishnupur in West Bengal and the temple of Vitthala in Pandharpur in Maharashtra. Manipur, whose princess married Arjuna, has an important Krishna temple. Their importance lies in the fact that Krishna is believed to have appeared to devotees in these places.

Kerala's tradition of Krishna worship stems from the association of the Pandavas who are believed to have spent the last year of their exile incognito at Thiruvarrpu. Guruvayoor, Mavelikara, Ambalapuzha and Kaladi (birthplace of Adi Shankara) have large Krishna temple complexes.

Udipi on the western coast of Karnataka is the home of the famous Udipi Shri Krishna temple consecrated by the thirteenth century philosopher Madhava. Before entering the temple, the devotee looks through the famous Kanakadasa kindi (window). Kanakadasa was a low caste devotee who was not permitted to see the image, although he spent many a night and day singing in praise of Krishna. Eventually, his devotion was rewarded, the wall cracked open, enabling Kanakadasa to peep in and look upon Krishna. Saint Vadiraja later installed a window in his honour. Udipi is also the seat of the eight Pejawar maths, one of the largest religious schools dedicated to Krishna.

Krishna and Rukmini are enshrined as Panduranga Vitthala and Rukmani at Pandharpur in Maharashtra.

An elderly couple—Jnanadev and Muktabai—had an only son called Pundarik who was selfish, led a dissolute life and was uncaring about his parents, who he sent out of his home. But his lifestyle made him both poor and diseased, so he became a wanderer till he met the sage Kukkut, who revealed that his strength and powers came from caring for his parents. Pundarik saw the light and rushed home to serve his parents without a thought for anything else. His piety brought Lord Krishna to him, disguised as a visitor, but as he was massaging his father's feet, he threw a brick outside and asked the visitor to wait on it. Later, he apologized when he found that it was Krishna, but the god pronounced his pitrubhakti (filial devotion) the highest form of devotion. The deity 'stands-on-a-brick' (Vitthala) waiting for his devotee Pundarik. The temple belongs to the Varakari Sampradaya school of philosophy whose greatest exponents were the saints Jnaneshwar, Tukaram and Namdev.

At Puri in Orissa, Krishna is represented as Jagannatha, accompanied by his brother Balabhadra and his sister Subhadra. The story goes that king Indradyumna commissioned the divine carpenter Vishwakarma to carve the images out of wooden logs. Vishwakarma agreed on condition of total isolation for a month. But the eager king could not wait and entered the workshop before the month was over. He found the unfinished images and had to consecrate them as they were.

But there is probably an earlier tribal association, for the images look very tribal. It is known for its annual chariot festival when the three gods are taken around Puri in enormous chariots (whence the word Juggernaut) with their aunt Gundicha, where the local people can worship them.

In the story of Krishna and the *Mahabharata* war we see the beginning of the internecine warfare that was to plague northern India for the next three thousand years.

Balarama

Some Vaishnavas believe that Balarama was the eighth incarnation and Krishna the ninth. This stems from their refusal to accept the Buddha as a manifestation of Vishnu.

But the *Mahabharata* and the Vishnu Purana say Balarama was an incarnation of Adi Shesha, son of Kashyapa and Kadru and the constant companion of Vishnu.

Balarama was born of an embryo transferred from Devaki to Rohini, another wife of Vasudeva. He was born in Gokul and was an inseparable companion of Krishna, as was his earlier incarnation Lakshmana of Rama. Balarama accompanied Krishna from Gokul to Mathura and took part in the wrestling competition, killing Kamsa's star wrestler while Krishna killed Kamsa himself. He too had miraculous powers and assisted Krishna in the destruction of the demons. He killed the ass-demon Dhenuka, the monkey-demons Dwivida and Pralamba. One day, his companions asked him to shake down fruits from trees belonging to Dhenuka, the ass-demon. Balarama obliged them, earning Dhenuka's wrath. The demon attacked him, but was easily killed by Balarama. On another occasion, the monkey-demon Dwivida annoyed Balarama who was talking to his mother, so Balarama killed him.

Balarama was well-known for his addiction to wine and his bad temper. Once, when he was intoxicated, he told the river Yamuna to come to him, so that he might bathe. The river refused. Furious, he threw his plough into the river and dragged her after him wherever he went until she begged for forgiveness. He also killed Krishna's brother-in-law Rukmin in a drunken brawl. Balarama had one wife Revati, who bore him two sons.

Balarama was an expert at wrestling and club combat. He taught Duryodhana, the Kaurava prince, and Bhima, the Pandava, to fight with the club. He did not take part in the *Mahabharata* war but on the day of the mace battle between Bhima and Duryodhana, he went to watch the encounter. Draupadi had sworn that Duryodhana would be killed by a blow to his thigh, so, as they fought, Krishna reminded Bhima of her vow.

But blows below the waist were forbidden, so Balarama, disapproving of Bhima breaking Duryodhana's thigh, left the scene of the war.

Balarama is associated with the plough, which he often used as a mace in battle, hence his name, which means 'Rama with the plough'. He is also associated with the pestle and the club, a weapon which he was an expert at using.

Balarama's character comes out as straightforward, fun-loving and highly principled. Krishna's machinations are beyond his comprehension and approval.

He dies along with his brother and Krishnavatara comes to an end.

Balarama is enshrined in the Puri temple in Orissa, along with his brother Krishna and sister Subhadra. Separate shrines to him also exist at Gokul in Gujarat, Alwaye in Kerala and Imphal in Manipur.

Buddha, the Preacher
of Peace

Considering the antagonism between Buddhism and Brahmanism, how, when and why the Buddha became an incarnation is a mystery. He is included in the Bhagavata Purana's list of manifestations, thereby authenticating his association. The inclusion was obviously an ingenious strategy to integrate a very popular religious cult into the mainstream Vedic tradition. While Buddhism, as a separate cult opposed to Hinduism, disappeared from the country, it is not certain whether Buddha's elevation to the position of avatara was responsible for this.

The Bhagavata Purana says that Buddha's birth was for the purpose of deluding and thus destroying the enemies of the gods. He assumed a mortal form in order to preach heretical doctrines in the cities founded by the demon Maya and in Kashi (Varanasi).

According to the Skanda Purana, the rains had failed for six successive years and famine stalked the land. Brahma approached Ripanjaya, king of Kashi, and asking him to change his name to Divodasa (meaning servant of the gods), told him that should he become king, the gods would shower the earth with rain. Divodasa agreed on condition that Brahma would assist him and all the other gods would leave the earth so that he could rule without any rivals. Brahma agreed and with difficulty persuaded Shiva to leave Kashi.

Divodasa ruled well, but the gods were angry at

their exclusion. Shiva sent his messengers to Kashi, but they were so happy there that they did not return. Then Vishnu, accompanied by his spouse Lakshmi and his mount Garuda, went and settled in Dharmakshetra, near Kashi. There he took the form of Buddha while Lakshmi took the form of a female recluse and disciple. Garuda became Punyakirti, a disciple to whom the Buddha taught the various branches of natural and supernatural religion.

Vishnu, as Buddha, taught that the universe had no Creator and that there was no Universal Supreme Being. Brahma, Vishnu and Shiva were merely mortals like himself. Death should not be feared, as it was only a peaceful sleep. Pleasure was the only heaven and pain the only hell, and liberation from ignorance the only happiness. Sacrifices were acts of foolishness. Punyakirti spread these messages in the city, while Lakshmi taught the women that all happiness was to be found in the sensuous pleasures of the body, and that caste distinctions were a figment of the imagination. As Lakshmi was very influential, her teachings spread rapidly.

As a result of the Buddha's teachings, which corrupted the people and took them away from the performance of rituals, Divodasa became dispirited. Then Vishnu took the form of a Brahmin and visited him. Divodasa narrated the many instances by which good men had to suffer because of the power of the gods and asked the Brahmin how he could achieve final happiness.

Vishnu told him that his insistence on Shiva leaving Kashi was the cause of all his troubles and advised the king to consecrate and worship an image of Shiva. Installing his son as king, Divodasa followed Vishnu's advice and worshipped the Shiva linga. Pleased, Shiva appeared and led him to his heaven Kailasa.

After converting Divodasa, Vishnu, as Buddha, stopped his heretical teachings and disappeared into a deep well at Gaya.

But the Buddhist texts tell a different story and one that dates to an earlier period.

The Buddha was born (in 483 BC) as Prince Gautama, son of the king of Kapilavastu and his wife Mayadevi, and belonged to the Sakya clan. His mother died seven days after his birth and her sister, another wife of the king, brought him up. As a child, he preferred meditation to play. So his father married him at an early age to his cousin Yashodhara. Although they were happy, Gautama would still meditate on the problems of life and death. The king tried to divert his thoughts, but without success.

Three incidents took place when Gautama was twenty-nine years old, which were to change his life forever. On one occasion, he saw a decrepit old man, suffering and ignored by his relatives. On another he saw a sick man, shivering and covered with mud. On the third, he saw a dead body. Gautama was shaken and felt that youth, health and happiness were irrelevant if they were merely waiting for old age, sickness and death. Then he saw a mendicant, one who had renounced all desires and led a life of austerity. Deciding that such a life was fulfilling and preferable, he slipped out of the palace late one night and left to seek the truth.

Gautama's journey of discovery took him to Brahmans and sages, through severe austerities and penance, none of which gave him his answers. Finally, under a pipal tree, he received enlightenment and came to be known as the Buddha.

The Buddha then proceeded to Kashi where he started preaching his philosophy. He travelled around the region of Kusinagara, Kapilavastu, Rajagriha and Vaishali, exhorting people to throw off the yoke of Brahmanic observances and follow the path of right conduct. He converted his own father, while his wife became his first female follower. He lived till the ripe old age of seventy, when he attained Nirvana in the city of Kusinagara.

Buddha's teachings were based on the Upanishadic philosophy of the transmigration of souls or Nirvana. Pleasure and pain depend on one's karma or actions. Existence is a misery, and death is not necessarily redemption. He taught four 'noble truths': pain exists; desire is the cause of pain; pain can be ended by Nirvana; removal of desire leads to Nirvana. He spoke out against caste distinctions and all those who followed his tenets became part of a great brotherhood. Rather than physical mortification or costly sacrifices, he taught that charity or love was the greatest virtue, leading to Nirvana. He did not speak of God or a 'Supreme Being'.

Later, Buddhist literature created an elaborate mythology around the Buddha. Buddha's victory over temptation was personified as the nullification of the attempts of the demon Mara (also described as the God of Evil or the Lord of the World of Passion) who tried constantly to tempt or kill him. Rama's battles with several demons including Ravana, Krishna's battles against an even greater number and Buddha's defeat of Mara were all part of a recurring theme: the triumph of good over evil.

Buddha's followers followed a practice of erecting stupas or tombs over the various parts of his body and later, those of his disciples and senior preachers known as Boddhisattvas. The stupas became the focus of popular worship and dot the eastern and western countryside. The main stupas are to be seen at Sarnath and Sanchi and the important temple is at Bodh Gaya. It is believed that the Buddha's tooth is preserved at Kandy in Sri Lanka.

As Buddha had warned his followers against worshipping his image, symbols of the Buddha, such as the pipal tree, his footsteps and the wheel of law were worshipped in the early period. Later, in the second century AD, the image of the Buddha himself was worshipped. In the absence of a god, Buddha filled the slot for his followers. To Buddhists, he was the sole god who came to earth to teach them the true path. To Hindus he became an incarnation of Vishnu, one of the many deities of the Hindu pantheon.

There is no doubt that Buddha contributed greatly to the Brahmanic religion he sought to cleanse. Sacrifices virtually disappeared from Brahmanism. Love and charity became ideals to be followed for a better future life for the soul, in preference to desire and sacrifice. Ahimsa or non-violence caught the imagination of the people, even to the later detriment of the country, making it susceptible to attack and conquest. His philosophy was the Upanishads put into action.

The Buddha's establishment of celibate orders of monks also had a profound influence. Adi Shankara, who probably lived in the seventh century AD, established similar orders in five different places. Although several religious orders came up all over India, the Shankaracharyas were to become the most powerful authorities of contemporary Hinduism.

Buddha's life and teachings dramatically changed the complexion of Hinduism. His invaluable contribution to this process undoubtedly earns him a place among the incarnations of Vishnu.

Kalki, the Final Destroyer

This is the tenth incarnation, which has yet to come. Kalki is expected to destroy evil and re-establish virtue, peace and prosperity. The age we live in—Kali Yuga—is named after him.

The Vishnu Purana gives a prophetic description of Kali Yuga.

In Magadha will come a ruler named Vishwasphatika, who will destroy the race of Kshatriyas and elevate fishermen, barbarians, Brahmins and other castes to power. Outcastes and barbarians will rule the Indus, Darvika, Chandrabhaga and Kashmir. The rulers will be wicked and violent. They will kill women and children and take away the property of the people. They will rise and fall rapidly, and will not be pious. While the devout are neglected, those who mingle with the usurpers will follow their example.

Prosperity and spirituality will decrease and the world will be depraved. Property alone shall confer status, wealth will be the only reason for loyalty. Passion will be the only bond between men and women, the latter being used for mere sensual gratification. Litigation will be successful by the use of falsehoods.

The earth will be venerated only for her mineral treasures, the sacred thread alone will distinguish a Brahmin (not his acts of piety). Dishonesty, weakness, subterfuge and threats will rule the day, gifts will be made on ordinary occasions, not on religious occasions.

Marriage will be performed out of mutual consent (i.e. love) and a person's clothes will decide his status. Water from afar will be deemed holy (not, as it should be, all fresh water).

It further predicts that people, unable to bear this, will go back to living with nature and eating natural foods, exposing themselves to the sun, wind, rain and cold. Life expectancy will come down and decay will flourish till the human race is annihilated.

When Vedic practices and the rule of law cease to exist, and the end of the Kali yuga approaches, the child Kalki will be born in the family of Vishnuyashas, a Brahmin of Sambhal village. He will destroy the barbarians and thieves and re-establish the rule of Dharma or righteousness. But those who change their minds and behaviour will be given a fresh chance and become part of a new age of purity, the Krita yuga.

Sculptures and paintings of Kalki show him to be a man on a white horse, sword in hand. Worshipping Kalki is difficult, for he has yet to reveal his form.

Other Incarnations and Manifestations

Although Vishnu is popularly perceived to have ten incarnations the number of manifestations changes from Purana to Purana. A list of twenty-two names is to be found in the Bhagavata Purana:

- Purusha, the progenitor of all creation, the original eternal man, even the Supreme Being. It is also another name for Brahma.
- Varaha, the boar.
- Narada, the sage, who has a leading role in the stories of Krishna. Some RigVedic hymns are ascribed to him. He is described as a Prajapati and a son of Brahma. Narada invented the vina (lute) and was the chief of the gandharvas (heavenly musicians). He was regarded as a mischief-maker, carrying tales from one side to another. But he was also a great writer on law and the author of the Naradiya Dharma Shastra.
- Nara and Narayana, the duo of the human and the divine, the doer who draws sustenance from the Supreme.
- Kapila, another great sage who was the founder of the Sankhya School of Philosophy. When accused by the sixty thousand sons of Sagara (the ocean) of stealing their father's horse earmarked for sacrifice, he reduced them to ashes with a glance. But when Sagara's grandson Anshumat appealed to Kapila to

raise them to heaven, he promised that Anshumat's grandson Bhagiratha would achieve this by bringing the river Ganga to the earth.

- Dattatreya, an incarnation of Brahma, Vishnu and Shiva, though primarily of Vishnu. He gave Kartavirya, a demon who worshipped him, a thousand arms. He had three sons, Soma, Datta and Durvasa, who also obtained some of the divinity of the Trinity. Dattatreya's three heads represent the Trinity, while he is accompanied by four dogs representing the four Vedas.

- Yajna, the sacrifice, who was personified as the deer-headed son of Ruchi and husband of Dakshina. He was killed by Shiva's son Virabhadra at the sacrifice performed by Daksha, son of Brahma, and a Prajapati.

- Rishabha, a great king of yore, the father of Bharata and founder of Jainism. He was the son of Meru and Nabhi and the father of a hundred sons, including Bharata. Leaving his kingdom to his son, he led a life of severe austerities and penance, wandering through western India till his death. He was the first Jaina Tirthankara.

- Prithu, a king of the solar race, believed to be the first person to have been installed as king. He was the son of Venu, a wicked monarch, and was born out of the right arm of the corpse of Venu, who had been beaten to death for his wickedness. Prithu granted life to the earth, hence her name Prithvi. He granted her a calf and milked the earth for grains and vegetables, on which people subsist.

- Matsya, the fish.
- Kurma, the tortoise.
- Dhanvantari, the divine physician, who taught the science of healing, or Ayurveda. He was produced during the churning of the ocean. He is also listed among the 'nine gems', nine brilliant men of the court of King Vikramaditya who lived in 56 BC. (His name appears twice in the same list.)
- Narasimha, the man-lion.
- Vamana, the dwarf.
- Parashurama.
- Vyasa, the author of the *Mahabharata*.
- Rama.
- Balarama.
- Krishna.
- Buddha.
- Kalki.

Other Puranas include the following incarnations:

- Hamsa, the mythical swan. Who Hamsa was or what he did is not known.
- Mohini, a combination of Shiva and Vishnu, who

charms the demons into forgetting the nectar of immortality during the churning of the ocean.

- Dharma, the learned and wise bull, who is also regarded as a Prajapati. He had numerous children who were personifications of morals, intelligence, virtues and religious rites.
- Sanata Kumara, the mind-born son of Brahma. He was a rishi and the author of a minor or Upa Purana, the Sanata Kumara Purana.
- Hayagriva, a form taken by Vishnu to recover the Vedas, which had been carried away by two demons.
- Mandhata, who established the duties of the various castes.

The Bhagavata Purana goes on to add that the incarnations 'are innumerable, like the rivulets flowing from an inexhaustible lake. Rishis, Manus, Gods, sons of Manus, Prajapatis are all portions of him'.

There are several manifestations of Vishnu unique to their regions. They contribute to the character and nature of the benevolent god who comes down to earth from time to time to help his devotees in distress.

- Vaikunthanatha is very popular in Kashmir, Himachal Pradesh and other parts of the Himalayan region. He has four heads: those of a man, a woman, Narasimha and Varaha. This form is worshipped in some temples such as the Hari Rai Temple at Chamba in Himachal Pradesh.

- Ranganatha is the god of the island (aranga) of Srirangam, formed by the river Kaveri and its tributary, near Tiruchirapalli in Tamil Nadu. Here Narayana rests on the serpent couch with his consorts Shridevi and Bhudevi at his feet. The Srirangam temple is a principal centre of the South Indian school of Vaishnavism, and was an important centre of Ramanuja, the tenth century Vaishnava preacher.

- Varadaraja, the giver of boons, is very popular in the south and is the main deity of the temple of the same name at Kanchipuram in Tamil Nadu. While the deity's right hand blesses the devotee in the abhaya mudra, the left arm points down, palm facing outward, in a gesture signifying 'take'.

- Padmanabha is often seen on temple walls as Narayana, from whose navel issues a lotus with Brahma seated on it. The Padmanabha temple at Trivandrum in Kerala houses this deity, who is also the patron god of the former state of Travancore.

- Balaji or Venkateshwara, the deity of Tirumala-Tirupati. He is a benevolent god, believed to always help his devotees when they appeal to him. Balaji is probably the most popular and definitely the richest deity in India today. The stories of his miracles are endless and draw multitudes of people. The crowds at Tirumala are proof of his popularity. Several new temples to Balaji have come up all over India. This is why he has often been described as the god of Kali yuga.

There are millions of temples to Vishnu and his incarnations and manifestations all over India. Many are local forms of his incarnations, as described in earlier chapters. Only some of the best known have been described here.

Lakshmi

Lakshmi is the consort of Vishnu and is also known as Shridevi. Sometimes Vishnu appears with one consort, Lakshmi or Shridevi, and sometimes with two, Shridevi and Bhudevi, the earth. Lakshmi is the Universal Mother, eternal and omnipresent.

The word Lakshmi means good fortune in the Rig Veda. Lakshmi and Shri are two wives of Aditya, or the sun, according to the Taittiriya Samhita, and issued out of Prajapati according to the Shatapatha Brahmana. Later, in the Epic period, she is the goddess of prosperity and the wife of Vishnu.

Lakshmi's origin is first described in the *Ramayana*. The story of her birth is narrated in the tale of the churning of the ocean by the gods and the demons. As they churned the sea of milk for the nectar of immortality, many fabulous things came forth.

After the appearance of the cow Surabhi and Varuni, goddess of wine, came the divine tree Parijata, the apsaras or celestial nymphs, the cool-rayed moon and then a terrible poison. Finally rose Shri, seated on a lotus. Her appearance was so wonderful that the sages were enraptured, the gandharvas (heavenly musicians) sang and the apsaras danced. Shri is described as young, gentle-eyed and beautiful, shining like a pearl with a golden sheen, bedecked with jewels. She is the queen of the gods, holding a white lotus in her hand and seated on a lotus. She is Kshirabdhi Tanaya, 'daughter of the sea of milk'. Her other names are Lakshmi, goddess of beauty and wealth, Padma, the lotus or Padmaja, the lotus-born, Jaladhija, the ocean-born, Chanchala, the fickle one, Shri or prosperity and Lokamata, the mother of the world.

The *Ramayana* also says that Lakshmi was born by her own will in a beautiful field opened up by the plough, hence her name Sita.

The Vishnu Purana says that her first birth was as the daughter of Bhrigu and his wife Khyati. She was born of the sea at the churning of the ocean in a subsequent birth.

Vishnu's ability to protect has eight aspects and these are known as his Shakti. Each aspect is depicted as a goddess. They are:

* Shridevi, goddess of wealth and prosperity
* Bhudevi, the earth
* Saraswati, learning
* Priti, love
* Kirti, fame
* Shanti, peace
* Tushti, pleasure
* Pushti, strength

Whenever Vishnu incarnates himself on earth, Lakshmi too manifests herself, in order to assist him.

The Vishnu Purana says that if Vishnu takes a celestial form, Lakshmi appears as a divinity; if he takes a mortal form, then she too becomes a mortal. She accompanies him constantly, whether in heaven or on earth.

Thus Lakshmi is Mother Earth who is saved by Varaha. She is born from the lotus as Padma in the Vamana avatara and as Dharani, wife of Parashurama of the Bhrigu race. She is Sita or Maithili, wife of Rama, found by King Janaka of Mithila as he was ploughing the fields. She is also Rukmini, wife of Krishna, and Yashodhara, wife of the Buddha.

Lakshmi may be two or four armed, generally seated on a white lotus and holding a lotus in her hand. Seated on an eight-petalled lotus and flanked by two elephants pouring sacred water over her, she is known as Gajalakshmi. In this form, she is sometimes depicted with gold coins pouring out of her hands. Sometimes the owl or uluka is her vehicle. Uluka is another name for Indra, the king of the gods. Thus prosperity rides the heavens.

Shridevi and Bhudevi

One aspect of Lakshmi is Shri—fortune or prosperity. Another is Bhu or Prithivi—earth—a name she receives from Prithu, son of Vena and the first king to have been installed on earth.

According to the Vishnu Purana, the sages made Vena king of the earth, but he was wicked and banned rituals and worship. So the sages beat him to death. But the world still needed a king, so the sages rubbed the thigh of Vena's corpse, and his sins came out as the evil Nishadas. Then they rubbed his right arm and out came Prithu, who was crowned king of the universe.

Meanwhile, famine was ravaging the land. So the people approached Prithu and asked him for the plants that the earth refused to yield. Prithu threatened the earth, who took the form of a cow. Prithu 'milked' her, making her yield numerous varieties of grain and vegetables. The earth is described as a cow and the milking is symbolic of the extraction of agriculture and prosperity. Because he granted her life, Prithu is the earth's father; hence the name Prithivi.

The word Prithivi itself means broad, signifying the wide world or the earth. She is the mother of all beings and is invoked along with the sky. There are three earths corresponding to the three heavens. Our earth is Bhumi or Bhu or Prithivi.

In some stories, Lakshmi's birth from the ocean is preceded by that of her sister Alakshmi, the personification of misfortune. As she is the elder, she is also called Jyeshtha, the name of a constellation as well. She is sometimes known as Mudevi. Alakshmi's function is to emphasize that good and bad luck go hand in hand,

and both are divinely ordained. The devotee must abjure those actions that will summon Alakshmi and focus on those activities that will attract Lakshmi.

What draws Lakshmi? Light, cleanliness, virtue, charity and peace are important to attract her into a home. The absence of one or more of these brings Alakshmi instead.

Lakshmi poojas or prayers to Lakshmi are performed to receive her blessings at home and at work. Business communities, especially traders, invoke Lakshmi before any important event and even on a daily or weekly basis. Deepavali, the festival of lights and a national holiday, is a time to invoke Lakshmi with lights, crackers and gifts.

Lakshmi is the protector of married women. She ensures the husband's long life and safeguards the woman's mangalya, which is prosperity linked to the life of her husband. In the southern states, a very important ritual called Varalakshmi pooja is performed by women. They worship the face of Lakshmi—either painted on a wall, depicted on a pot or made of brass, silver or gold and attached to a pot. The pot is filled with rice and is decorated with mango leaves and coconut, the goddess is bedecked with jewels and beautiful silks. Varalakshmi is invoked to ensure a long life for the husband and to avoid the stigma of widowhood.

Radha

The growth of Vishnu worship is undoubtedly related to the popularity of Rama and Krishna. Rama's spouse Sita is a daughter of the earth and, thereby, an aspect of Bhudevi herself. Krishna has two consorts, Rukmini and Satyabhama, identified with Shridevi and Bhudevi.

But there is one other—Radha. It is difficult to say when she actually appeared, or when her cult came into being. She is non-existent in early literature, unknown to the Vishnu Purana and the *Harivamsha*. The amorous sports of Krishna and the gopis (cowherdesses) are first mentioned in the ninth century Bhagavata Purana, but Radha is still not mentioned. There is, however, mention of one who was a favourite of Krishna. She is mentioned in Hala's *Saptashati* and in a verse from the Dhanvyaloka of AD 580. Nimbarka, who lived in the twelfth century, probably introduced the cult of Radha. According to Nimbarka, Radha was the eternal consort of Krishna who lived with him in Vrindavan. The popular cult of the love of Radha and Krishna first appears in the *Gitagovinda* by Jayadeva who lived in the court of the Sena king of Bengal, Lakshmana, in the twelfth century. But southern Vaishnavism ignored her totally. So, who was Radha? Was she a creation of a devotee's imagination? Or did she exist? We will probably never know.

Vaishnavism

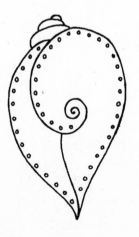

Vaishnavism is the name of the cult of Bhakti or devotion that recognizes Vishnu as the sole or Supreme God. This cult of devotion to a personal god originated in the pre-Christian era and first developed in the Tamil country, in the songs of the Alvars and Nayanmars, Vaishnava and Shaiva saints respectively. The word bhakti first appears in the Upanishads and refers to a form of worship whereby God is attained only through absolute and whole-hearted devotion. The devotee relinquishes all religious rites in favour of prapatti, or total resignation to his god, in order to attain moksha or liberation.

Presenting a marked contrast to the ritualism of the Brahmanas, the philosophy of the Upanishads and the atheism of Buddhism, this was a religion that celebrated God as a divine figure of love and grace, protecting his followers and responding to their prayers. Shiva or Vishnu became the focus of the devotees' absolute devotion.

In the Vedas, Indra is the supreme deity while Vishnu is a mere associate of the rain god. It is only in the Brahmanic period, probably after the association of Narayana, that the cult of Vishnu grows, suggesting the pre-eminence of the non-Vedic Narayana, who combined with the Vedic Vishnu. The identification of Vishnu-Narayana with popular hero gods such as Rama and Krishna contributed to the pre-eminent position of Vaishnavism. Further, in his several incarnations, Vishnu is identified with numerous local deities, many beyond the pale of Hinduism. By absorbing them within himself, he increases his acceptability and the number of his followers.

Bhagavata

The greatest philosophy associated with Vaishnavism is contained in the Bhagavad Gita, the Song of the Lord, where the divine Krishna expounds the philosophy of action for the sake of good, without thought of reward, and total devotion to a personal god.

The Bhagavata cult, born of the worship of Bhagavat Vasudeva Krishna, Vishnu's incarnation in the *Mahabharata*, and belief in the philosophy of the Bhagavad Gita, was an early form of Vaishnavism that rose in the Mathura region of north India.

The Bhagavata dharma is a monotheistic creed demanding absolute love or bhakti for the Supreme Being or Bhagavat. Prapatti or complete resignation to god leads to moksha, or liberation of the soul. The Bhagavata cult stresses that divine grace alone can confer knowledge and wisdom.

The Bhagavatas rejected differences of caste, sex or birth, thus paving the way for the inclusion of a large number of adherents. Many Greek kshatrapas (satraps) of north-western India who had followed Alexander of

Macedonia to the east became Bhagavatas. Among the early archaeological remains of north India is a second century BC pillar erected in honour of Vasudeva by his devotee Heliodorus, a Bhagavata. Thus the religion had begun to gradually supplant Buddhism as the religion of the land.

The Gupta rulers of the fourth century AD were devotees of Vishnu and adopted Garuda as their emblem. This provided a major impetus for the growth of the Bhagavata cult. The Guptas were an imperial power and their patronage was responsible for the growth of this cult all over the country.

Vaikhanasa

An early and important sect of Vaishnavism, Vaikhanasa, attributed to the philosopher Vikhanas, is mentioned in the Taittiriya shakha of the Rig Veda. However, in the north, it did not reach the popularity achieved by the Bhagavatas. The cult figures prominently in Chola inscriptions and thereafter. The Vaikhanasas were the hereditary trustees of Vishnu temples in south India. Even the rise of Ramanuja, the great Vaishnava preacher of South India, and his efforts to convert the rituals to the Pancharatra school to which he belonged did not succeed in dislodging the Vaikhanasa agama which, despite the small number of adherents, is still followed by more temples than the Pancharatra agama.

According to the Vaikhanasas, Narayana is both formless and with form, the two being inseparable. Lakshmi is his ever-present potential shakti, assuming different forms to suit his different manifestations. The Vaikhanasas disagree with the Bhagavata school, which believes that God can dwell in the devotee's heart. For the Vaikhanasas, serving the image of the God is the primary duty. They do not worship saints or monastic heads, nor do they brand their bodies with Vishnu's emblems like some other Vaishnava sects. Their rituals are conducted only in Sanskrit: they do not recite prayers in the local languages. Today, they are a small sect restricted to Tamil Nadu, Andhra Pradesh and Karnataka.

Pancharatra

A more widespread school of Vaishnavism is the Pancharatra ('five nights', an uncertain epithet). There are early (seventh century AD) records of acrimony and doctrinal differences between the Bhagavatas, known as Vishnu-bhakta, and the Pancharatras, known as Vishnu-bheda.

Vasudeva Krishna and his family are identified with five cosmic emanations called the vyuha (conditioned spirits). From Vasudeva, the Supreme Godhead, developed Sankarshana, another name for his brother Balarama. The two are invisible to the human eye. This emanation took place at the beginning of time and was identified with prakriti or primal matter. The two produced Pradyumna, Krishna's son, who was manas, the mind, from whom arose Aniruddha, Krishna's grandson, identified with ahankara or self-consciousness. Then the three gunas or traits evolved, and with them Brahma, the Creator. Later, another Vrishni hero who was a son of Krishna—Samba—was identified with the vyuhas and the four became five. The five aspects of the Supreme Being Vishnu are para (the formless, invisible Supreme), vyuha (invisible, lying in the ocean), vaibhava (the manifest incarnations), antaryami (not visible but making its presence felt), and archa (iconic).

In the Pancharatra system, the soul is one with the Supreme, but is also an individual. Even in a state of salvation it retains the individuality to realize the bliss of union with the Supreme. The Pancharatra school was born in Kashmir between the fourth and eighth centuries. It found its fruition in the Bhakti cult of the Tamil Alvars and the later Vishishtadvaita of Ramanuja, who preached qualified monism, whereby the soul is one with god yet separate.

Alvars

A new form of devotion for a personal God—Shiva or Vishnu—developed in the Tamil country. It included concepts of love, sin and a sense of inadequacy. The devotee expresses his love or devotion for Vishnu, combining the love for a parent, spouse, sibling and child. Vishnu responds by absolving the devotee of his sins and granting his wishes. The devotee feels inadequate, that he has not surrendered totally, and strives harder to serve and love Vishnu better.

The Alvars were Tamil devotees of Vishnu. There were twelve of them—eleven men and one woman—who lived between the third and eighth centuries. Each is associated with miraculous events in which Vishnu protects his devotee. They composed sublime poetry that came to be known as the 4,000 Divyaprabandham. The Vaishnava Alvars, along with the Shaiva Nayanmars, were the chief propagators of this new form of devotion—bhakti to a personal god. They preached in Tamil, which was to become the forerunner of popular religion, by which local saints composed prayers and preached in their local languages and dialects.

The first three Alvars are Poygai, Bhutam and Pey, names meaning spirits. The fourth, Thirumalisai, was a yogi. The greatest was the fifth, Nammalvar, who wrote four major poems—Tiruviruttam, Tiruvasiriyam, Periyatiruvandadi and Tiruvaimoli—also known to the Vaishnavas as the Tamil Vedas. Nammalvar's poems have contributed greatly to the shaping of southern Vaishnavism. The sixth Alvar, Kulasekhara, was a king of Malabar who retired to Srirangam, where he lived in pious poverty and composed beautiful poetry in praise of Vishnu. The next Alvars were Vishnuchitta or Periyalvar and his daughter Andal. The last three were Tondaradippodi, Tiruppanar and Tirumangai.

The Alvars wrote emotional, rather than metaphysical, devotional verse, choosing the path of self-surrender, which is open to all people regardless of birth.

Acharyas

A new age of Acharyas or teachers who based their teachings on both Sanskrit and Tamil texts followed the Alvars in the south. They considered it essential to follow the three paths of devotion, action and knowledge in order to reach the truth. They were orthodox Brahmins who established the rituals, festivals and observances that were followed by later Vaishnavism.

The first of the Acharyas was Natha Muni, son of Ishvara Muni, a Pancharatrika who founded the family of Tatacharyas who laid down the codes of Vaishnavism. Natha Muni saved the Divyaprabandham from oblivion and introduced them in the temples, thereby giving an equal status to Tamil. He was appointed the first Acharya or pontiff of the Srirangam temple.

The next great Acharya was Natha Muni's grandson, Yamunacharya, who established the orthodoxy of the Pancharatra school.

But the greatest of the Acharyas was Ramanuja, who lived in the eleventh century and whose father was a disciple of Yamunacharya's grandson.

After Ramanuja's time the southern school of Vaishnavism split into the Vadagalai or northern branch promoted by Vedanta Desikar, and the Tengalai or southern branch promoted by Parashara Bhatta and Periya Achana Pillai. There were several doctrinal differences between the two, one of them being the choice of language. Sanskrit was preferred by the Vadagalais, whereas the Tengalais preferred Tamil. The Tengalais admitted adherents from all castes, even converting them to the Brahmin caste. Their differences became irreconcilable to the extent that they even fought in court over which caste mark was to be worn by the temple elephant—a matter finally decided by the Privy Council in London!

The Vadagalais established the Ahobila Math and a system of Jiyars who provided spiritual leadership. But the Tengalais, by preaching in the local language and admitting all castes, took their religion to the people and gained greater popularity and followers.

Ramanuja

Born in AD 1017 in a Brahmin family, Ramanuja wrote commentaries on the Upanishads, Brahma Sutras and the Bhagavad Gita. While he accepted the importance of rituals and the supremacy of the Upanishads, he maintained that the highest form of salvation was that attained through bhakti or devotion to Vishnu and the abandonment of one's self to him, putting trust in his grace and compassion. His philosophy was called Vishishtadvaita or qualified monism with a personal god who is Vishnu. As opposed to the pantheistic and neutral Brahman of Adi Shankara's Advaita (monism), Ramanuja advocated a personal deity who rewards devotion with salvation. Further, according to Ramanuja, the individuality of the soul is preserved even after moksha or liberation.

Ramanuja's ideas formed the basis of later devotional sects of Vaishnavism all over India. Apart from expounding his philosophy and writing his commentaries, Ramanuja was a great organizer. He appointed seventy-four spiritual heads to popularize the Vishishtadvaita school of Vaishnavism. He converted several non-Brahmins and encouraged them to wear the sectarian marks, dress as Vaishnavas and observe Vaishnava customs. He also converted several rulers, such as the Yadavas and Hoysalas, to Vaishnavism, thereby ensuring royal patronage for his religion.

Madhava

In the thirteenth century, Madhava, born in the Kanarese country, broke with the Upanishadic tradition and began to preach dvaita or dualism. He made a distinction between god and the soul and believed that Vishnu saves those who live pure and moral lives, while the evil are destined for eternal damnation. He also brought in the devotee Hanuman, as an agent for the Lord's grace.

Jayadeva

He was a Bengali poet who lived in Kenduli during the reign of the Sena king, Lakshmana, who ruled in the last quarter of the twelfth century. Jayadeva composed charming and lyrical poetry in a form which he named padavali. The immortal *Gitagovinda* and the *Ashtapadi* were composed by him. He promoted a religion of love based on the passionate story of Radha and Krishna.

Chaitanya

Shri Chaitanya lived in Bengal between AD 1485 and 1533. He spent his early years as a scholar and teacher. Bengali Vaishnavism originated with Madhavendra Puri Gosvamin, who taught his disciple Ishvara Puri Gosvamin, who in turn initiated Shri Chaitanya.

Vrindavan became the centre of Bengali Vaishnavism in the north and Puri, where Chaitanya spent his last years, in the south.

Chaitanya travelled around the country—from Rameshwaram in the south to Vrindavan, Varanasi and Prayag in the north, and Ramkeli in Bengal—preaching the greatness of Krishna and converting people to his religion. He spent the last eighteen years of his life at Puri in Orissa, identifying himself with Radha, beloved of Krishna.

According to Chaitanya, Brahman is infinite and all-pervading, with supernatural powers and attributes. He is Krishna, and all other names and deities are but manifestations of Krishna. Krishna's human form is really infinite and all-pervading, perfect and enchanting. His abode is Vrindavan, which became the focus of the Chaitanya cult.

Chaitanya classified devotees into four types: dasya bhaktas or loving servants, sakhya bhaktas or friends, vatsalya bhaktas or parents and kanta bhaktas or beloved devotees. The last form is the highest and Radha is the foremost of these devotees, represented by the gopis. This love is often mistakenly identified with carnal desire. The relationship between Krishna and the gopis is the ideal of unrestricted love between two lovers. He elevated passion to a high spiritual plane.

Shri Chaitanya attached great importance to the

constant chanting of Krishna's name, listening to narrations of his lilas, living in an atmosphere of devotion to Krishna, residing at Vrindavan and worshipping the image, believing it is the Lord himself. Humility, tolerance, strict vegetarianism, honesty and above all, love, are essential in a true believer. Total and universal love for Krishna and service towards all living beings comprise the only path to realize the Ultimate Reality.

Towards the end of the seventeenth century arose the Sahajiya sect, which opposed the Gosvamins. This sect propagated the involvement of several women in a man's life, non-vegetarianism and no self-discipline. It culminated in the Vairagi-Vairagini sect, which brought the Chaitanya cult into disrepute and to its nadir. This cult has more or less disappeared in this century.

Shankara Deva

Shankara Deva lived between about AD 486 and 1568 in Ali-Pukhuri in the present Nowgong district of Assam. He travelled all over India and, after studying the different schools of Vaishnavis, returned home to preach.

Shankara Deva was deeply influenced by the Bhagavad Gita, on which his teachings were based. He emphasized that bhakti, or total devotion, was the only path. Mahapurusha, or Vishnu as the Supreme Being, and kirtanas, or songs in praise of god, were the method of worship. His mantra for initiation was a simple *Hare Rama Hare Krishna*. Unlike Chaitanya who saw the love of a consort as the supreme form of devotion, Shankara Deva emphasized that dasya bhakta, or the love of a servant, implying service without thought of reward, was the greatest.

Shankara Deva faced great opposition from the Buddhist Tantrikas. However, the Koc king Naranarayana and, later, the Ahoms adopted his teachings, thus establishing an Assam school of Vaishnavism based on bhakti and sankirtan.

The teachings of Chaitanya and Shankara Deva also spread as far as Manipur where Vaishnavism established a firm foothold.

Vallabha

Vallabha was a Tailanga Brahmin from Bellary, Karnataka, who lived in the sixteenth century. He preached the cult of Krishna, the beloved of the gopis, and Radha, his consort. This cult evolved elaborate rituals, festivals and feasts for the worship of Krishna. The emphasis was on sportive enjoyment coupled with morality.

This sect gives an exalted position to the guru or spiritual guide who is known as the maharaja. God can be worshipped only in the home or temple of the guru.

Worldly life is no bar to salvation and even the gurus were married men who led worldly lives.

The Vallabha sect was popular among the merchants of Gujarat and Rajasthan, where it continues to flourish.

The cult of Vitthala

The medieval saints of Karnataka and, later, Maharashtra, were ardent devotees of Vitthala of Pandharpur, a manifestation of Krishna seen along with his consort Rukmini. Although Pandharpur is now in Maharashtra, it was formerly part of the Vijayanagara empire and later passed into the hands of the kings of Mysore. Krishnadevaraya built a temple to Vitthalaswami in his capital (now Hampi in Karnataka). Vitthala was the object of adoration of the Dasa kutas or Haridasas (slaves of god) who were inspired by the teachings of Madhava in the thirteenth century. The cult can be directly traced to Narahari Tirtha, Madhava's disciple, and Shripadaraja, the head of the matha of Padmanabha Tirtha at Mulbagal in Karnataka.

The early devotees of Vitthala wrote their songs in the Kannada language, extolling Krishna or Vitthala who could be reached by wisdom (jnana) and devotion (bhakti), self-discipline and a very high standard of ethics. The Dasa kuta saints took on a synonym of Vitthala as a mudraka or pen name as an expression of their devotion and humility.

The famous saints of this cult who composed in Kannada were Sripadaraja, Vyasaraja, Purandaradasa, Kanakadasa, Vadiraja, Vijayadasa and Jagannathadasa. The Dasa system expounds the Dvaita or the philosophy of duality propounded by Madhava. But it was not a philosophical cult as much as a movement for religious revival. The songs are lyrical and didactic rather than logical.

The saints who wrote in Marathi included Jnanadeva who wrote the *Jnaneshvari*, a commentary on the Bhagavad Gita, in AD 1290. The devotees of Vitthala include Namadeva (end of the fourteenth century), Ekanatha (end of the sixteenth century) and Tukarama (seventeenth century) who described their mystical experiences and visions of Vitthala in a musical form known as abhangs.

Medieval Vaishnava mystics of North India

With the advent of Islam and the corresponding religious upheaval, a great need was felt to seek the truths of the Hindu faith. It was Ramananda who founded the movement to achieve this goal. He combined philosophical concepts with the bhakti movement and the idea of prapatti or surrender that had established itself in the south. Although not many of his compositions remain, his teachings live on in the compositions of the first twelve disciples who were drawn to his ideals.

Ramananda preached the ideal of one god who made no distinctions on the basis of caste and creed. Although his god was Brahman, many of his followers were devotees of Rama or Krishna. Mirabai, the Rajput princess, was an ardent devotee of Giridhara or Krishna, in whose name she composed beautiful verse. Namadev of Maharashtra was his follower, while Tulsidas was a devotee of Rama and composed the *Ramacharitamanasa* or the *Ramayana* in Hindi verse. The blind poet Surdas composed devotional poetry to the child god Krishna.

There were many other local Vaishnava saints who between the thirteenth and eighteenth centuries tried to reconcile the differences between Islam and Hinduism by preaching of one god who did not see differences of caste and creed. Rama or Krishna became symbolic of this single god who could be reached by unswerving love and devotion. The saints were mystics who, by sharing their personal experiences of Vishnu or one of his aspects with the people, contributed greatly to the spread of Vaishnavism.

Diffusion of Vaishnavism

Music and dance have played an important role in spreading the cult of Vaishnavism. Poets composed soulful songs of love and devotion. Artists explained the *Ramayana* and *Mahabharata* in a mixture of prose and poetry, known as Harikatha. The epics were translated into every language for easy access and comprehension by all. The Vaishnavas made a point of singing in the vernacular languages, thus popularizing the religion.

Another means of popularizing their beliefs was through jatras, performances of mythological plays and stories taken from the Puranas. The jatras invariably demonstrated the victory of good over evil and were an important means of establishing moral order. The Ramlila of northern India, the jatras of Bengal and the Yakshagana of Karnataka are some examples of these performances. An extension of this was the puppet shows which narrated the tales of Rama and Krishna.

Sankirtanas were assemblies of people who sang kirtanas or religious songs in praise of their diety. The Divyaprabhandam of the Tamil Alvars, the kirtanas of Jayadeva and Chaitanya and the abhangs of Tukaram are some examples of the passion poetry of the Vaishnava saints who reached out to touch the hearts of the common people by praising Rama and Krishna in song.

Finally, sculpture and painting also acted as signposts to reach Vishnu's heaven. The miniature paintings of the Rajput period portrayed the tales of the child god Krishna and his lilas. Temples were adorned with sculptures and paintings that were intended to increase interest and faith in this creed.

Conclusion

Vishnu is as old as Indian culture. He is worshipped all over the country and has been a common ideal and force for regions as diverse as Rameshwaram and Vrindavan, Dwarka and Manipur.

The identification of Vishnu with the popular hero-gods Rama and Krishna has undoubtedly aided his growth and popularity. Rama and Krishna are the binding forces of Hindu culture, as they depict the social and moral values of Hindu society. The epics are known in every part of the country and form an integral part of the upbringing of every child. As manifestations of Vishnu, Rama and Krishna lead to the ultimate goal of reaching Vishnu's paramam padam or lotus feet.

The use of the arts—music, dance and drama—to spread the tales of Rama and Krishna has increased their popular value. People enjoy sitting through long nights of music and drama, puppetry and dance, all of which are utilized to spread popular Puranic stories.

Vishnu's ability to absorb local deities has also helped to enhance his acceptability. People and cults that would have otherwise stayed outside the pale of Hinduism were gradually assimilated into this popular religion.

Finally, the worship of Vishnu demands bhakti, prapatti and sharanagati—or, total devotion, surrender and no thought of any other god. These are the paths to moksha, that liberate the soul from the bonds of earthly life and desire. The jiva or the individual soul achieves this through service and faith, one in which there are no distinctions of caste or creed. In the rigid caste-dominated structure of Indian society, this is a defining moment, when the individual is set free to traverse a new path, a path that will ultimately lead to Vishnu.